D1612750

VIEWPOINTS

VIEWPOINTS

POETS IN CONVERSATION

WITH

JOHN HAFFENDEN

FABER AND FABER
LONDON & BOSTON

First published in 1981
by Faber and Faber Limited
3 Queen Square London WC1N 3AU
Printed in Great Britain by
Redwood Burn Limited Trowbridge

British Library Cataloguing in Publication Data

Haffenden, John, *1950–*
Viewpoints.
1. English poetry – History and criticism
2. Poetics
I. Title
808.1 PR503

ISBN 0–571–11689–2

CONTENTS

PREFACE

This series began in January 1979, when Alan Ross showed enough faith to send me on my way to Dublin to interview Seamus Heaney for *London Magazine*. The other interviews took place between then and April 1980. As a book, the whole venture developed in consultation with Charles Monteith, whom I warmly thank for his enthusiasm and tactical assistance. The choice of poets is nonetheless my own.

We agreed on ten as the optimum number of poets for the volume, principally in order to allow each one sufficient space to develop his thoughts and arguments without unnecessary constraints. The length of each interview bears no relation to any judgement of relative merit or importance, however—only to the circumstances of the day and the time available for each conversation. Given the great number of contemporary poets in Great Britain and Ireland, it was obviously impossible to be comprehensive without creating an unmanageable book. In limiting it to ten inteviews, I am only too well aware and sorry that I could not include other poets whose work I find stimulating and valuable, but just as no critical weighting is implied by the proportions of each interview here, so I had no intention that any critical inference should be drawn from my omissions.

I should like to thank Alan Ross for his great interest and help, and for first publishing four of the interviews—Seamus Heaney, Douglas Dunn, Richard Murphy and Philip Larkin (all but the last in slightly modified forms)— in *London Magazine*; also Craig Raine, who published an abbreviated version of the Thom Gunn interview in *Quarto*. I am grateful too for help received from Jonathan Barker of the Poetry Book Society; Anthony Rota; and Eric Walter White; and for the shamingly efficient and intelligent typing assistance of Rosalind Duckmanton and Sue Hammond. My greatest thanks go to the poets themselves, whose uniform courtesy and consideration have impressed me most warmly. This book is dedicated to them.

Sheffield, June 1980 JOHN HAFFENDEN

DOUGLAS DUNN

You once wrote that you felt quite grateful to have been born at the bottom of the pile . . . Can you tell me about your background?

Because it's the kind of thing I'm concerned with in my writing, it seems to me more like a foreground. Inchinnan is the first countryside to the west of Glasgow; it's a very old village and parish—an ordinary, respectable, working-class background. There are still a lot of farms in Inchinnan, but the character and personality of the place has changed; it's no longer quite what it looked like when I was a lad.

My father's background is interesting: he was born in Halifax, though his parents were Scots, and went to work in a factory—India Tyres—which was a bit of an eyesore, but you took it for granted. My father's mother came from Aberdeenshire, and my grandfather, who died very young in 1922, came from a farming family in north Ayrshire. He was a carpet designer, quite a successful man; he worked for Templeton's in Glasgow, and then moved to Halifax to work for the big carpet company, Crossley's, and by all accounts became fairly bourgeois. He died when my father was about eleven. There seems to have been a substantial fortune, but my grandmother had a crooked brother who swindled her out of the largest part of her inheritance. My grandmother died when she was extremely old, a very majestic, dignified old figure.

On my mother's side, my grandfather was the cooperative baker in the town of Hamilton; a very kirkly man, an Old Left Socialist of considerable conviction. I know that side of the family much more intimately.

Were you a bookish child, reading Scott and Stevenson?

I didn't get very many children's books, but I think this is common at that level of society. My grandfather, who was a self-taught man, had quite a substantial library, and I used to look at his books, which probably made them think I was more precocious than I actually was. I suppose I was quite bookish, but I was also an outdoors boy. I went to primary school in Inchinnan, then to Renfrew High School, and finally to school in Paisley.

When did you start to write, or feel that you might become a writer?

Not until after my first book of poems did I feel I might become a writer. The tedium I felt when I was working in the University Library here reached such a pitch that I felt I could no longer write poems and do the job. It was then I decided that if I was a writer, I'd better be one. It took me until the age of twenty-seven or twenty-eight before I worked up enough confidence to actually accept that I could be a writer.

Did you choose librarianship as a career, or was it something you 'lapsed into'?

I think it was something I collapsed into. Leaving school with a pretty indifferent set of Higher Leaving Certificates . . . I didn't have enough to go to university, and I don't think it really crossed my mind; in any case, I didn't have the credentials. Much of the time I worked in branch libraries, in centres which would consist of a few wooden boxes of books put on shelves. I used to like working in Port Glasgow, a very industrial place, a shipbuilding town; there was a great deal of unemployment, and the unemployed are great users of libraries. We used to order Westerns and detective stories by the yard, never by the title. It was undemanding work, but it gave me time to read a lot. I've great affection for those days, because I really did enjoy it. Going to library school for a year's full-time education struck me at the time as being about my limit. When I started I was paid about £5 a week; when I qualified, it went up to about £8, and I decided it wasn't enough, so I caused considerable fury by leaving Renfrew County Library. They thought I owed them more time at sweated labour rates, something I didn't agree with. So I got a job in what was then the Royal College of Science and Technology, which became the University of Strathclyde while I was there. (Librarianship is in fact an interesting profession, not as dull as I sometimes make it out to be.)

We went to Akron, Ohio, when we married in November 1964 . . . but I got called up there (that's talked about in my poem 'The Wealth'). I keep my call-up papers inside Robert Lowell's *Selected Poems*. I went to the medical . . . and we left a couple of weeks after that. I had an immigrant's visa, though *I* thought I was an emigrant. Legally they had a right to conscript aliens after a year. It was 1965, and the Vietnam War was hotting up, and the Americans were caught without enough men and obliged to extend the Draft.

What had prompted you to go to the USA?

I felt very much outside the Scottish literary scene—to the extent that there actually *was* one then—and I thought my chances of publishing in Scottish magazines were very slender. It was also considered a good thing for a British librarian to get some experience in an American library. While I was in America, I decided I wanted to go to university. I did apply to Scottish universities, but they told me I had to acquire an 'Attestation of Fitness'— a Presbyterian-sounding demand—and they asked me to sit preliminary exams in subjects which were ludicrous. The chance of spending three years reading poems, plays and novels was quite tantalizing by then. When I was in America, most of the poetry I read was American poetry—Lowell, Berryman, Jarrell, and James Wright, for whose poems I've a particular fondness—and I got very interested in American things in general.

What degree did you get?

I got a first.

Did you ever think of undertaking postgraduate research?

I certainly considered it, but I thought I'd gone to university as a librarian and that I should take this 'new, improved' librarian back into librarianship. Also, my first book of poems came out in the year I graduated, in September 1969. I thought that if Philip Larkin, the University Librarian, could write marvellous poems and still be a librarian, then so could I. My ambitions lay in the direction of becoming a university librarian, but eighteen months in the Brynmor Jones Library put paid to that. My literary ambitions came out simply because they were being suppressed by the nature of the work I was doing.

In coming to Hull, did you find it necessary to define yourself as a poet against Larkin?

In my first summer here I worked as a dogsbody in the library's cataloguing department, so I've known Philip for a long time. Perhaps if I hadn't met him I might have been tempted to define myself—for or against—in the way you suggest. I can certainly get pissed off by being referred to as Hull's 'other poet'. So if that's happening, I don't need to do it myself. His encouragement has certainly meant a great deal to me.

Ian Hamilton wrote about Terry Street *that you offer 'convincing sketches of at least the surfaces of humdrum urban living',*[1] *which has always struck me as a rather backhanded compliment . . . would you accept that characterization of the book?*

I don't think I would characterize it in that way. The word 'urban', for example, is not really applicable. A little street like that is more like a village; it's contained very much within itself. Each little enclave like that within a city has a status of its own which it defines in its own terms, a little community.

We lived in Terry Street—in a cul-de-sac called Flixbro Terrace, Terry Street—for almost two years. It's now demolished; the last time I was down there, there was an encampment of gypsies or tinkers, large chrome caravans, a fire burning in a brazier. It's waste ground now, and presumably the corporation will build new houses there, which is what I think they ought to do, instead of moving people out to monolithic estates.

Had it become a sort of earnest of your belonging to the street to observe and commemorate the place?

I didn't see it in that light until after I had left Terry Street, even until a long time after the book had come out. I think it was a more selfish—certainly subjective— exploration than anything outgoing towards Terry Street and the people who lived there.

[1] *Observer*, 7 December 1969.

The posture you adopt is that of the spectator, isn't it?

Not just a spectator, but something of an outsider, because I'd never lived in a district like that before. And I was also a Scotsman among a universally English population. And I came from a messily semi-rural kind of background, and this, Terry Street, and Hull were quite different. When I was in America, I had felt that the people you met, the places they went—bars, diners, streets and shops—everything looked so much more characterful (I'm probably misleading myself into thinking that) than what I'd known in Glasgow. Since then I've come to think that Glasgow is the most characterful place I've ever known or ever will know. I found that exciting when I was in Akron, and I was just thinking about coming to grips with it, thinking about it as an outsider perhaps, when we had to leave. After we'd been in Terry Street, I began to see it as characterful, too, and stimulating to my imagination in the same way as America had been. So I think possibly my poems about Terry Street are poems I should have written about the village I'd come from, and possibly the poems I might have written about Akron if I'd stayed there just a bit longer, except that the objects of observation would have been quite different. My imagination had been encouraged by the work of writers like Sinclair Lewis, Anderson and Dreiser, who are very social writers.

To what extent did you really feel involved with Terry Street ... in the poems you seem to have a way of imputing motives which is possibly presumptuous for an outsider?

To a large extent I think I was offended by their complacency: that is, towards the environment. The street was in a Tory ward of the town. There were things that would rub my back up the wrong way about the place, and in particular the way they had accepted all the paraphernalia of pop culture, and the extent to which a large part of their lives had actually been formed by that; the way in which things I myself am interested in had been excluded by pressures which didn't come from our common culture but from other sources. I found that disturbing. I was conscious of writing about that, as in the first poem of the book, and not about Terry Street, but about the country as a whole. I think perhaps the poem which says most about this is 'The Silences'—'It is baked now over their eyes like a crust'—which I think is true.

How then would you describe the feeling you had towards the street . . . as one of concern, or what?

No, I don't think so . . . it was much more relaxed and much more personal than that. To a large extent the novelty of that street to me was a handicap, it was so new and strange. In any case, I'm not the sort of person who would want to urge people to put up barricades at the end of the street . . . I'm a civilian.

Latterly you've set a great deal of store by a sense of commitment to a place. What is the nature of your own commitment?

I think my main commitment to place is to the place I come from; to some extent my expression of Terry Street was a surrogate, a substitute, for my commitment to somewhere else.

Did you feel, to put it crudely, that you were exploiting Terry Street to some extent?

No, absolutely not. I think I can be confident in saying no to that, because the poems arose so gradually and naturally to me. It was a release, because if I'd followed deliberations which I'd been going through before then—wanting to write about Scotland—I would in fact have been forcing it. In Terry Street everything was there to be seen, and what I saw and experienced recommended itself to me in the form of poem: I just obeyed my imagination.

In some of your essays you've spoken of the word 'objectivity' in a very special sense, as connoting sympathy. For most people it might mean not necessarily disinterest but dispassionateness, whereas for you it seems more giving?

I think so. A word I might use in this context, in preference to objectivity, would be passivity, in the sense that Orwell uses the word in his essay 'Inside the Whale' when he's talking about Henry Miller's novels; which is not passivity in the way it would be used in contemporary humbug as a put-down—that is, not being 'active' enough—but the writer allowing his own mind to happen in the face of other things that were happening round him.

In one poem, 'Men of Terry Street', you remark that 'they are too tired/And bored to look long at comfortably': do you think that was a true observation?

I think it's a true observation of a very large sector of the British working class: the same sector perhaps that votes people like Margaret Thatcher into power ... a kind of defeated resignation before the facts of their own existence—facts which, to a large extent, they don't recognize. But I admit, too, that it was me who felt uncomfortable.

Did you have any sense at all that you were using local folk to illustrate a thesis—as representative of an urban condition?

No, I don't think so. I mean, the deliberation that went into the writing of the poems could be greatly overrated, and at certain times I have felt tempted to rewrite these poems and introduce motives I didn't have when I wrote them. I think I wrote Terry Street unself-consciously and what they add up to, if anything, is a matter for the reader to decide. I certainly didn't organize any particular thesis.

At times you're very sharp and censorious, as when you term Hull a 'city of disuse, a sink' ...

Well, in a flat town like Hull which is built upon mud, the very foundations of the town can, in certain moods, seem to ooze up through the splits and cracks in the pavement ...

... and into the very psyche of the people?

That's an occult generalization it's very easy to leap to, since you don't need any evidence, you just draw conclusions. But I think at certain times in writing those poems—I possibly flatter myself by saying—I could perceive something as general as that. I was very stimulated during the period I was writing them, over about a year, and it was an unhappy period to some extent, too, because at certain points I was surrendering to the moods which certain sights and so on were engendering in me. In other words, the subject matter began to possess me, which is something I've never felt since to anything like the same extent ... over a number of poems. I have felt that with individual poems, and therefore it doesn't last very long. But when it lasts for a long period, you feel a certain gratitude in having been possessed by the objects of your concentration for so long.

You manage to be both tender and gentle in those poems; were you chary of sentimentalizing at all?

Well, when we were talking about my background, one of the things I didn't mention was the Presbyterian part. I still am a closet Calvinist, and I was then too, I suppose. Probably I was making quite self-conscious efforts to reject it then, which I've since given up: you are who you are. The kind of mentality you inherit from the religiosity to which you were exposed as a child is—in my case, because it was Presbyterian—a state of mind which induces the ability to be sentimental, as well as the hard-headedness which fights against sentimentality, with a consequently caricatured ruthlessness. I think that's one of the main tensions within Scottish literature. The phenomenon you get in the literature of the late nineteenth century, and at the turn of the century in Scotland—it's called the Kailyard—is a luxuriating in sentimental, rural, small-town life ... I think it grows out of John Galt's novels and short stories, *The Annals of the Parish* and so on... Since then Scottish literature has shown an antagonism towards the sentimentality which swamped it in the late nineteenth century. As a Scots writer I've always been aware of the possibility of lapsing into sentimentality, and I may well have nodded ... I can't help it, it's just part of my nature. And the rest of the time, perhaps most of the time, I'm fighting against it. In *Terry Street* obviously I'm running that kind of risk, although I daresay English readers of *Terry Street* wouldn't really be aware of that; I think some Scottish readers might.

In the last of the Terry Street *poems, 'A Window Affair', you say that 'in this time, this place,/There is a house I feel I have to leave,/Because my life is cracked ... And does not want to love, and does not care.' Can you elucidate that ... were you actually rejecting the street?*

I think I would be as blunt as that, yes ... the fatigue that it induced in me, and the passion with which I actively resented what the material I had been writing about had done to me: that is, introducing a kind of physical tedium, a depression of one's own horizons. Half the time I kept worrying whether the rain would come in, or whether little damp marks on the wall would grow to be big damp marks; the discomfort of the place had become much more tangible and visible, which it hadn't been during the time I was writing poems, but by then I'd written them.

There's another poem in the volume, called 'Landscape with One Figure', set by the Clyde, where you figure yourself as 'An example of being a part of a place' . . .

Yes, it's where I come from, the south bank of the Clyde, from which you can see what used to be John Brown's Shipyard. I *could* say that of there, but I couldn't say that of Terry Street. My commitment to the landscape of that poem is significant to me, whereas my commitment to Terry Street was just temporal: I did happen to live there, that's all. A couple of years after leaving Terry Street, I did have an active dislike of Terry Street itself and all streets like it, and especially of the kind of society which allowed such streets to exist. Since then I've developed a sincere and genuine affection for what the place meant to me, if only out of gratitude—it gave me a subject for a book of poems. Until then, quite frankly, I didn't have any subjects. Like most poets I'd tried to sound a thousand years old, as Chesterton says young poets are prone to do. Keats never really had a subject but a point of view, a way of addressing himself to a subject that was almost entirely nebulous. I did have a subject there; I did have things, objects, people, a way of life: things that one could observe and be submerged in. I can only be grateful for that. I can see my former neighbours in a slightly different light, as being perhaps more independent, having more dignity than I gave them credit for. It's very much a young man's book of poems, I think, a first book. I often wish I could go and do it again.

You often used the words 'rot' and also 'silence'. Silence seemed to be an emblem of what you were looking for . . .

If you like, it's the silence of civilization, of urbanity, civility, and things in good order. 'Rot' may be applied in the same way.

Yet you deplore what you've called the 'impotent urbanities' of Auden, for instance?

I believe in urbanity, but I deplore complacency and fellow-feeling towards a few like-minded people: I think it's a failure of goodwill, if nothing else, if you don't aspire towards a larger number.

In a bulletin for the Poetry Book Society, you call Terry Street a place of 'sad sanity ... an alternative to the gaudy shams everywhere' ...

That might appear to contradict what I've just said, because of the extent to which I found the people infected by popular culture. I think since then I've got my ideas a bit more sorted out. The closer I was to Terry Street the less able I was to articulate what I felt about it apart from in my poems ...

In the reference book Contemporary Poets, *Maurice Lindsay is very severe on your next book,* The Happier Life, *when he says 'The Terry Street Room-at-the-Top Dunn becomes, in* The Happier Life, *his second volume, Life-at-the-Top Dunn—and all he seems to want to do is snipe and sneer at everything that comes within range...'*[1]

I think to understand his point of view you'd have to have an insight into the nature of Scottish literary politics ... the fact that I'm a Scotsman with self-conscious Scottish interests, though I don't live in Scotland, and I don't know the majority of the people in the Scottish literary scene. W. S. Graham has been consistently neglected in Scotland. I haven't abnegated my own country; I don't have an English accent and I don't think like an Englishman. I think Irish writers, and certainly English writers, tend to be much more secure in their identities than Scottish writers, and to them this sort of thing must look comic and perhaps even pathetic. You are made to feel it, even if temperamentally you're not interested in picking up plaudits on the grounds of your nationality.

How would you now estimate the poems of The Happier Life*?*

I think the first poem, 'The Garden', stands up all right by my own expectations of my work. The syntax in the last verse gets lost, and it's a poem that I've wished I'd rhymed. There are other poems—'Supreme Death' and 'The River Through the City'—which have what I think are some of my best lines. 'Bird Poet' and 'Fixed' pleased me well enough at the time, too.... Poems like 'The Hunched' and 'Under the Stone' are rather similar to *Terry Street*, but they're too general to be set in Terry

[1] James Vinson (ed.), 2nd edn, St. James Press, 1975, p. 405.

Street. There's a seam of these running through the book.

Were you ramifying what you'd first felt and expressed in Terry Street*?*

Reviewers felt that I was setting off on a different tack, trying to write a book that was self-consciously different, and I don't think that was the case. There are no poems in *Terry Street* which are written in rhyme and metre, and there are rhyming couplets and stanzas and so on in *The Happier Life*. I think Colin Falck said I was trying my hand to show that I could do it; but even before *Terry Street* I had been writing in rhyming verse, and I had begun 'Morning Bedroom', for example, before *Terry Street.*

At the end of 'Syndrome', you ask, 'What is the best? Not idleness, not careers./The only answer is to live quietly, miles away.' Did you believe that?

I believed it then, but I don't believe it now. At the time I was trying to assert the rights of ordinariness, the beauty of the average.

What would you believe now?

Searching for truth. The reason I would have made that sort of conclusion to a poem comes from a distaste for public life, a distaste for the flaunting of self-confidence. There are much more particular expressions of that: one poem, 'The Sportsmen', for instance, rises from a repugnance for competitiveness within public and private life, the ethos of sport applied to politics and to domestic life. That kind of thing annoys me a great deal: people not living as people but living as competitive entities, and trying, pathetically, to be heroes.

A lot of what you write expresses distaste for many things, which implies an idealism. Can you tell me what your idealism consists of?

An aspiration towards justice: a dream of equilibrium, good order, benevolence, love, of the kind of sanity which men have it within their means to create. I think the phrase 'private enterprise' is a good summary of what I detest. When freedom to buy and sell becomes the primary freedom in our society, which it is, and when that freedom is asserted as being more important than any other notion of freedom, then I think we're living with a set of false priorities. There is a larger freedom, which I think my work is interested in putting above the freedom to buy and sell.

The freedom of the imagination is surely bigger and more potent than the liberty of shopkeepers to do as they like.

In 'Midweek Matinée', you remark that drunks show 'What happens to men who are not good at life', and end up by saying, 'I can't stand what you bring out into the open.' One might see a disdainfulness in those observations.

I would dispute the disdainfulness, and I'd claim the lines are true. It's true that when you see such individuals, that's what you resent them for, the fact that the state of being miserable and benighted is so obvious. They're almost boasting their misery; you resent them for the kind of feelings they induce in you. Having grown up near Glasgow ... the sight of such low deprivation, the sight of people having reduced *themselves* to it as much as having *been* reduced to it by other things, has always impressed me and always moved me. I've been drawn towards that ... and it's not *nostalgie de la boue*. When you live in a place like Hull, you're *in* the *boue*, there's no need to be nostalgic for it. *Nostalgie de la boue* is a middle-class syndrome, common in people who never saw the social mud when they were young. I've seen it all my life, and I've always been drawn to it ... even in a kind of *fin de siècle* way, perhaps. My imagination is drawn to it, it's not a political choice or anything like that. I still have the belief that these people know truths that I don't know, and I'd like to know what they know.

Does indignation possess you as much as—or more than—any other emotion?

I don't think it's indignation: it's a combination of affront and also of resignation. I'm sufficiently realistic to know that simply being angry about these things doesn't contribute a great deal towards changing them, nor does any other political ideology. Judging by recent reviews of my latest book, *Barbarians*, I think my political commitment has been grossly overstated. I think the twentieth century has been a tale of humiliation, and that British society is so complacent that it doesn't realize the extent to which it's been implicated, adding to and compounding this humiliation with its own behaviour ... the way in which certain people must live—stood on by other people.

In the poem 'The Happier Life', which is presumably the fulcrum of that volume, you say, 'Community's a myth. We'll never find/The men whose happier lives and peace of mind/Outstay all changes, all rises in income,/ Resisting the pretensions of the scum.' You have in mind a world of the imagination, but something we might aspire to?

A kind of crystal ... bejewelled urbanity—much, I imagine, like the notional civilization that the Greeks and Romans had, where ours is based upon greed. They did have a dream, which I don't think we have. I think the poem suggests that the man who wrote it has some dream of perfection which in the poem he reduces until all he's left with is what happens in the last lines of the poem, which is substantially a transferral from actuality to the inorganic world, minerals and rain. That's the thing to which I, in my dilemma, transfer myself by the end of the poem.

So you'd say that commitment can be ineffectual, despite a sense of disturbance or resentment?

There are times when I wish I wasn't really concerned with these subjects at all, and that I could just simply relax and deal with the play of phenomena and experience in my imagination, in a much more leisurely and perhaps 'poetical' kind of way, rather than be concerned with subjects which—on the surface at least—are so recognizably social. There are times too when I've thought I'd work through these subjects in the hope of getting rid of them, working them out of my system, so that I could start to become a different kind of poet. I like writing about trees, for example ... As a person I'm very much on the side of life, on the side of potential for happiness and growth and fulfilment, all the good things. But the way in which I end up writing some poems is by the *via negativa*, which to me seems the only appropriate way of dramatizing my testimony. To do it from purely lyric motives, in confrontation with various phenomena, natural or otherwise, is to me dishonest, and evasive, when I have other things on my mind which I'm condemned to remember. I would like to work towards the position where it wouldn't be, but I realize that there would have to be changes in society and the whole foundation on which our society is based before that could happen. I tend to use physical reality as a way of objectifying something which is contentious; that is, something that some people would say was negative. Other people might say it was positive, depending on which side of the political fence your beliefs fall. I don't *like* it like that, but for me it would be dishonest to do otherwise. Anyway, I can't help it. In my third book, *Love or Nothing*, there are poems about trees. 'Winter Orchard', for example, started with, I hope, a physical and sensuous evocation of a particular tree—a pear tree I had at that time—and it ended up as a mysterious allegory . . .

You can manage a very plain vehemence, can't you, as when you call some people 'scum'?

I do tend to think there are bad people, and that we shouldn't mince our words.

The group of 'Barbarian Pastorals' (in Barbarians*) is possibly as outspoken as you've ever been?*

Yes, but the outspokenness is strategic . . . The poem 'Gardeners', for example, was meant to express a Lawrentian philosophy of nature, if you like: the gardeners see themselves as being in obedience to the earth, not to the man who owns it. It's a poem against property, and it does indulge in a certain amount of grand guignol towards the end—it's a theatrical piece, and its outspokenness is contrived in that way, too.

'An Artist Waiting in a Country House' has quite a different character . . .

In my first draft I was under the impression that I was writing a poem about patronage, and the differences between now and then, but a good deal of that got lost in the way the poem unfolded. By the time I finished, what I'd done was a very different poem, in a completely different mood from when I started. It's not a matter of changing my mind, but of discovering the nature of what my mind is as far as a particular poem is concerned. I think the imagination is very mysterious; you're never quite sure how it's going to produce during the act of writing. In *Barbarians*, after I'd written the first couple of poems, I did realize what I was up to, and that wasn't nearly as natural and relaxed a performance as *Terry Street*; I did deliberately organize *Barbarians*. There are three other poems I've written since the book, including 'Tannahill' and 'John Wilson in Greenock' [*Akros*, vol. 13, no. 39, December, 1978], which should be in the first sequence of *Barbarians*, and I perhaps published the book too quickly.

Do you feel that the critics who've been severe on you have somehow misapprehended what you're trying to do?

I think in this book it's probably my fault; if I'd waited a bit longer and included these other poems, then I think the stylistic gambit of that section of the book would have been much clearer. Also, having written about a place like Terry Street, people leap to the conclusion that I am, as the man in the *New Statesman* said, 'Red Dunn'. And although I'm left of centre, I'm not so way-out as all that; I'm probably closer to being a wishy-washy liberal than I am a Trotskyite. I take my political bearings largely from the past, which I regret; I wish I could be a little bit more present-day-minded about these things. I've always admired my grandfather, who was Old Left; he's the man in the poem 'Watches of Grandfathers'. The part of Scotland I come from has a pretty wholesale Socialist tradition, but to me that's a mythical politics. Yet that Clydeside mythology means a lot to me in terms of my imagination and I associate it with my own notional craftsmanship—'Clyde-built'. I don't really put much store upon the political meanings of my poems in terms of political reality. A lot of my politics is drawn from the mythology of Red Clydeside, from my family background, and from my own actual background in the place where I grew up.

'Barbarian Pastorals' is very Scottish, very local, and I think the three other poems would have emphasized that to a greater degree. Tannahill was a sad case; by all accounts a competent weaver, he wrote songs and began to pick up the threads, so to speak, of Burns's work. As a young man, he made a pilgrimage to Burns's birthplace, a two days' walk ... that kind of mythology means a lot to me, self-indulgently perhaps. Tannahill's reputation grew, but he was unpopular among his contemporaries; he knew more than they did and seemed to be tendentious on literary matters among his fellow weavers, and when his book came out, his friends didn't think much of it. Some of his songs became very famous. He was a self-conscious literary artist, and his ambitions lay in high art, not folk art, and since he came from Paisley he was the first poet for whom I could feel some kind of fellow-feeling, and who suggested to me that I could do it too. He committed suicide in the River Cart, and on my way home I had to cross that river. Quite a few times I walked part of the way with my English teacher, who was always talking about Tannahill, and he showed me the culvert where Tannahill had committed suicide. He drowned himself with his poems, and they were fished out of the water the following morning. I was staggeringly moved by that story. The poem is about Tannahill, and not about me, I'd like to emphasize.

In a way the poem is a litany, isn't it?

Yes, I think so, but one of the main reasons why I wrote the poem is that it gave me the opportunity to write in Burns's stanza, which I'd never done before. Other poets—John Fuller and James Fenton recently—have used it in a high-spirited way, but it's an elegiac stanza, and I wanted to restore it to its previous dignity. Wilson wrote his poem 'The Clyde' in iambic pentameter couplets, so I used that form for 'John Wilson in Greenock'. I have two more poems to do, though I'm a bit suspicious about the enterprise. I want to write one about John Leyden, who introduced Raffles to the East India Company; he was a poet and philologist, a protegé of Scott's, and died in the Far East at the age of thirty-six. He was a surgeon and self-taught linguist, and he died in highly absurd fashion in Java . . . first off the boat, cutlass in hand, although the opposition ran away; but he died of pneumonia caught by wading through the sea. I'd like to write a poem about that kind of Scotsman—a lad o'pairts—who goes abroad and does exotic things and dies in an exotic manner. Cunninghame Graham, for example: one of the things he was looking for in Central and South America was a way of dying in an exotic way, I'm sure; that's a Scottish syndrome. I also wanted to write a poem about Alexander Smith, who wrote a marvellous long poem about Glasgow and another shorter poem about Edinburgh; considered a great promising figure, he also died very young, A great celebrity in his time, he wrote a couple of prose books, one called *A Summer in Skye*; a very fine poet, he's no longer considered even within the canon of Scottish literature for some reason which doesn't elude me—he was associated with 'Festus' Bailey's spasmodical school of poetry; that is, with English poets. Once I'd done those, I think I would have covered quite a large spectrum of the personalities, concerns and issues involved in Scottish literature—almost like a critical work.

Have you then come full circle, towards fulfilling a sense of being Scottish, and being able to compose upon Scottish issues and places?

I might seem justified in saying that, but I don't like looking for patterns within my own work. I dissociate polemics from the imagination, and all my interests are on the side of the imagination itself, rather than its themes and subjects. I realize that the imagination does what it must, not what it ought to do. Imagination is amoral. The moralism that I introduce into my imagination happens because of who I am; perhaps didacticism is in my imagination to some extent because of my background. When you grow up with a finger wagging at you, there comes a time when you want to wag it back! But I hope I've finished with that.

So you're answering to something in Scottish affairs or history that you haven't felt capable of before?

At the time I was writing *Terry Street*, I did *want* to write about Scottish things, but in Hull there was something recalcitrant, and fascinating, which became an obstacle between me and Scottish subjects. I still feel that obstacle, although I got rid of a lot of it by writing a television play, *Ploughman's Share*, and also a radio play called *Scotsmen by Moonlight*. There is a poem in *Barbarians* called 'Elegy for the lost Parish', and *Ploughman's Share* was to a large extent based on that poem, except that the ploughman is made into a different kind of man, with a wife and a son. The last line of the poem, 'Heartbreak and loneliness of virtue!', is the particular burden he has to carry. His ploughman's share is a can of shite, an ancient petrol can full of gunge ... even if you're on the side of the angels, you end up drinking the can of shite, which I think is, these days, realistic, though it may seem pessimistic. In an essay I defined optimism as a perverse operation of the will, and I don't admit to the existence of pessimism; pessimism is a psychopathological complaint. But there *are* things in your own personality which can darken your poems to a deeper shade of black than is really the case.

In writing about MacDiarmid, you've said, I think, that there's been too much of the political in defining Scottish literature.

What I've wanted is a release from the terms MacDiarmid laid down as the only ones for discussing Scottish history, politics and literature. I think any writer who is a Scotsman has to take his bearings from MacDiarmid because he's our only indisputable modern landmark. In Scotland, if you don't support the national team with quite the necessary barbarism you cease to exist. A Scottish writer has been obliged to be loyal to things in his country that he may perceive to be distinctly malignant; you owe allegiance even to the worst. I admit now to being a closet Presbyterian, a cupboard Calvinist, but at the time of writing *Terry Street* I was probably trying to spit on that every five minutes. Now I wouldn't bother, I know enough about myself to say, 'That's who I am.' There are dark, dirty things in Scotland to which I owe some kind of passive, perverse allegiance ... there are lots of Scottish writers who undoubtedly came round to that in the end, like Carlyle and Stevenson. I'm quite sure that MacDiarmid—for all his vaunted progressive Communism and scientific vision—I'm sure that deep down he knew he was a Lowland Presbyterian Scot of low horizons, and that his scientific sweep was an aspiration generated from having been brought up in a fairly suppressed kind of environment. The awful germ is there, you've got to guard against it ... but there are also beautiful things in having been brought up in that way.

Would you like to go back to Scotland?

Yes, very much. I think to a large extent it's inevitable, I don't think there's any point in postponing it. I know where I belong, where I should be.

Can you tell me about the interest or circumstances which inspired you to write a beautiful poem called 'Homage to Robert Desnos', which you published in London Magazine *in March 1979?*

Desnos often managed to write surrealist poems in rhyme and

metre, which I find tremendously exciting, and I think the kind of poet I'd like to be—if I could just get rid of the subject matter I'm shackled with, simply as a fact of who I am—is the kind Desnos was. He's one of my favourite twentieth-century poets. I think that in a sense that poem is much more characteristic of my imagination than *Terry Street*, or *Barbarians*, though I would find it hard to justify that statement . . . That line by Desnos which I quote in the poem, 'A widow in her wedding-gown gets into the wrong train', is surrealist but it carries with it a whole world of comment and narrative: to be able to write that kind of thing, that's my ideal. Desnos is classically European, too, like my other heroes, Camus and Nizan. Britain bores me.

You've written an essay on the work of George Mackay Brown where, if I remember rightly, you censure him for not allowing for 'the possibility of an Ideal Cosmopolis' . . .

I find Mackay Brown one of the best poets around; a remarkably interesting poet. I also find it significant that he lives on the edge of British society, which is both his strength and his weakness—he's an agrarian romanticist, I think. In my mind, the better community is in the future; in Mackay Brown's mind, it's in the past. My enterprise I suppose is to recuperate tolerance and benevolence, to preserve it into the time when technology produces the sort of cosmopolis that I think we're all going to live with, inevitably. I think that while Mackay Brown has a marvellous historical sense, he doesn't have any way of interpreting it in a social-historical way. He can depict history without that portrayal conveying the germs of its own revolution and reformation, although you know from other poems that he's interested in that reformation. He's even—in 'Fishermen with Ploughs'—reached the last word in censure: apocalypse, or armageddon. I don't get into that level of indignation, the 'Black Pentecost', as Mackay Brown calls it. I don't see the salvation of man lying in a preliminary holocaust: it demeans the ingenuity of man as well as his residual moral sense.

To what extent do you feel motivated by melancholy? Do you suffer from it, or thrive on it?

I thrive on it. Randall Jarrell had the courage of his melancholy and I think poets should have the courage of their temperaments. My melancholy is the effect my material has on me; that's what it induces.

You've denigrated common sense; why is that?

I'm a Francophile, I don't believe in common sense; it's an Anglo-Saxon virtue. Scotsmen, like Frenchmen, don't believe in common sense, we believe in intelligence.

And for the same reason, you throw out opinions and bad temper?

Yes . . . rubbish, no philosophical tradition behind them. I'm a ponderous thinker!

One critic of Barbarians *implied that you think too much, and that by doing so you were balking your inspiration . . .*

I don't think so. It was Martin Dodsworth in the *Guardian* who said I should stop thinking . . .

Do you understand the criticism?

Yes, I do, it means 'stop thinking', but I think it's characteristically English to expect a poet to pretend that all he has to do is feel. Thinking is the activity that goes on before the imagination works, so to speak, and it feeds the imagination, but the imagination uses it in a different way, not in the manner of logical thought . . . I'll keep thinking, thank you.

But you have said that the imagination can be menacing, which suggests that you could activate it in certain directions?

I think that's the kind of remark of which I might have been guilty about four years ago when I was reading lots of critical texts, and I was almost deliberately trying to politicize my mind. I stopped doing that simply because I thought it was a Coleridgean sort of thing to do, and you'd end up with no imagination at all. Sartre in 'What is Literature?' talks of the imagination as being social democratic . . . Social Democratic, Democratic, Socialist, Communist, Fascist, or anything: I don't think the imagination is vulnerable to being categorized like that, unless the owner of the imagination goes out of his way actually to make it fit these ways of describing it, and I've decided not to do that. About four or five years ago I did try to make my imagination fit a particular kind of description, but it didn't last very long.

But if we accept that the first section of Barbarians *has a thematic coherence which partly has to do with excoriating any sector of society that condescends to any other section, isn't that a way of programming the imagination, or of putting it to a cause in a similar way?*

Well, putting it to the cause of—not myself exactly, but to the cause of my experience, which is what most poets do with their imaginations.

Do you think that you're now largely moving away from writing poetry to writing short stories?

Well, I've always written short stories and, to tell the truth, in my late teens and early twenties, I thought I was going to be a novelist and a playwright before I was going to be a poet. I've been publishing stories since about 1972 or 1973, not many, but it's beginning to pick up.

Do you see a point when you might give up writing poems?

There are times when I'd quite like to give it up, since I find the poetry world distressingly combative. That's a temporal intrusion, it's an affront to my imagination which I think is a disinterested imagination despite the allegedly contentious things which it's spewed up in metre. In short stories I find I can relax much easier, simply because it's not poetry, and short stories—which are regarded as a minor and neglected genre these days—aren't surrounded by anything like the controversy that poetry or, for that matter, the novel or playwriting are surrounded by. So you have a little place where you can be absolutely yourself, and nobody gives any bother whatsoever—a sort of haven, a sanctuary, a place without the burden of theory and criticism. Because most of my poems are narratives, short-story writing comes very easily to me; my poems and short stories have been feeding one another in private for years.

I would very much like to do a novel; I've tried and done several drafts, all of which by my standards amounted to drivel. I see myself just as a writer, not as a poet, playwright or short-story writer. I think everything I've done is connected, all part of the same ripple, the same endeavour; they're all saying much the same thing. The attractions of doing a novel are obvious: it's a bigger ripple, more conspicuous than a poem or a story. I've got one which I think I'm going to finish, it's about two-thirds through the first draft.

It seems to me that in your short stories you find a lightness of touch, a generosity and gentleness, while in many poems there's much more animosity; is that a distinction you'd acknowledge? The poem called 'A Late Degree' (Barbarians), *for example, is in a sense a nasty poem, which you end by admitting that 'there is no vernacular of compassion'*. . .

Our language has got to a point where it's very difficult even to *describe* something in precise terms—simply because of the various pressures on the language—which leaves it very corrupt for exact literary use, and leaves it, too, without 'a vernacular of compassion'. I suppose that's a fairly unforgiving sort of poem, but what I hoped was that in the poem I had nothing but a kind of hopeless, ineffective sympathy for the woman (and for her husband for that matter), and yet perhaps also an ambiguous censure of her optimism, the fact that she actually thought she could get away with it—on her own terms, not on my terms. That was a poem I thought of writing as a short story. But many of my poems are like that, they could be short stories.

The critic John Bayley has called some poems by Auden and Hardy 'sung short stories': that's the condition to which I'd like some of my poems to aspire, 'Elegy for the lost Parish', for example, or 'The Musician' or 'Drowning'. You have to show things in a story; you have to show things in a poem too, but you can *tell* things in a poem. Strangely enough, we consider prose the language of telling, poetry the language of showing, but in contemporary poetry you can tell as much as you show. Sometimes you can show without telling, and that's preferable. Short stories are very close to the spirit of poems, like Chekhov's story 'The Kiss', in the feeling they impart to the reader. But I think you're quite right, and I think that what you see in my stories is really my reason for writing them. I mean, by no stretch of the imagination could I be thought of as a 'hard man'.

Who are the writers with whom you feel most affinity?

I find quite a close affinity with Derek Mahon's concerns, thematically and stylistically. I think we've gone through the same period of literary time, although we may have reacted in different ways to different dilemmas. And Michael Longley is another poet with whom I feel considerable affinity; the Scottish poet Stewart Conn; and Seamus Heaney too, to some extent. I can see the way their imaginations work more clearly than with other, older contemporaries ... Tony Harrison too, though I don't know him very well; Hugo Williams, Ian Hamilton, Tom Paulin and Glyn Hughes are others. I feel no affinity with MacDiarmid, though I have a lunatic respect for his work. He was a volcano, but his mind was totalitarian. He imposed rather than expressed.

In twentieth-century poetry it's very hard to take your bearings, and it doesn't matter which level of society you come from; it's very difficult to find your way by plotting courses from acknowledged figures. My own feeling is that you try to emulate the kind of effects that poems you've admired have had on you, more than you do the particular styles of individual writers. There are lots of ways in which I'd defer to Larkin—obviously he's a much better poet than I am. I think he might see himself as a traditional lyric poet who's got fucked up on the *realia* of his particular moment of the twentieth century, which has ruined the nature of his lyricism. I think Ted Hughes is probably a traditional English nature poet in his heart, but because of contemporary humbug, as well as the humiliations and upheavals of the twentieth century, and the distortions upon the imagination which they've produced—the affront of recent history—he's been deflected away from an attention to nature and creatures, which I think is his love, in order to orchestrate feelings within a kind of Lawrentian ideology: it shouldn't really be necessary.

How do you feel about the situation of poetry today?

In the last issue of the *Review* I confessed to feeling very hopeful indeed about the present situation in poetry. There were a great many poets around and I think I made the mistake of saying there were about fifty poets whose work could be read with interest. Now I feel a bit less hopeful, the number has dwindled, but that may be just my feeling. I certainly don't credit what a number of people call traditionalism—for instance, the way in which Roy Fuller understands it; I find that beneath contempt.

That gentlemanly verse, towards which poets like Philip Larkin and Kingsley Amis have tended, is highly regrettable, since I don't think they should grudge the nature of the imagination the spaciousness which it has.

Do you think, then, that there's something very wrong when the imagination is at ease with the social life?

I think in the perfect society the imagination *would* be at ease with the social life. In a rubbish society like ours, when the most to be hoped for is that imagination might be at ease with the physical self, then poetry becomes an act of private consolation; consolatory, too, to a handful of others, instead of social in a universal sense.

Do you now align yourself with any particular political position?

With an amorphous left wing: it's a left wing of the spirit, not just a political left wing. I stand, if you like, with the ghosts of my grandfathers. It's an antagonism towards the way in which people think about nature as well as about society . . . a politics of life, or of being, rather than a politics of politics.

THOM GUNN

I want to start by referring you to a remark you made some years ago to the effect that for a long time you had felt nervous and muted in giving readings of your poetry, but then you found the answer to the problem in dramatizing your readings. Did you feel that your poems needed a dramatic rendering for them to be understood and appreciated?

A poetry reading is kind of special, since for one thing you have to avoid your most difficult, compressed poems; you have to read poems that can be understood on a single hearing. For a few years I was just too nervous to be able to read well, but at a certain time I got so used to it I stopped being nervous. I learned how to give a reading—to pace it, arrange the poems, and to make remarks in between the poems, partly for explanation of the poem that is to come, and partly as a way of varying the poetry reading voice. I don't like actors reading poetry, but I'm so little of an actor and have such a comparatively unmodulated voice that the more dramatization I can manage the better, since there's no danger of my seeming over-dramatic. Yvor Winters, who wrote an essay on the subject, was in a peculiar position, because he had a most extraordinarily wonderful voice—the slightest modulation could sound very dramatic—so that when he read in what he thought was a monotone his voice was continually interesting. On the other hand Allen Tate read very badly, all on one note.

Could you explain what you meant when you wrote that poetry is a product of obsession?

Obsession is another name for passion perhaps. But you do have to be obsessed about something to write well about it. I'm often asked about the genesis of poems, and my answer is that I might begin just with an idea, really rather a general one—it might even be a concept, but you don't just sit down and write about a concept unless you're in the eighteenth century. The thing you want to write about—whether a specific scene, incident or idea—gestates, and the process of writing becomes an exploration. You discover things about yourself and about your insight into your subject matter that you didn't even guess at. The surprises that occur on the way are often the most exciting things about writing. Sometimes when a poem is going flat I realize it's because the poem has become an exposition of my original idea and no more. It is the discoveries that make the poem. I agree to that extent with writers like Robert Duncan who believe so in the improvisation of the moment. But my point is that the subject of a poem can only gestate if you are obsessed by it in the first place.

In the face of what you've just been saying, however, would you accept my feeling that there was perhaps too much cognition, too much premeditation, in your first two books, Fighting Terms *and* The Sense of Movement*?*

There is an awful lot of harping on the word 'will' in the second book, perhaps quite monotonously. That book struck me as almost didactic when I read it through again a couple of years ago—almost as though I'd set myself a programme. I was very influenced by Sartre, obviously, and in particular by a short book called *Existentialism and Humanism*, and I certainly kept close to that text the year or two I was writing *The Sense of Movement*. The second book seems particularly stiff to me, not so much the first book. There I was trying to be the twentieth-century John Donne, somebody I didn't discover until I was an undergraduate at about the age of twenty-one. Reading Donne was a tremendous explosion for me, and I think a lot of that first book, *Fighting Terms*, shows it. There are certainly worse influences, and I don't regret it: in fact I learned everything from it. I think one thing Donne taught me was what Frank Kermode calls the relationship between image and discourse, and to be able to accept discourse as a proper part of the poem in the twentieth century, as opposed to those both in England and in America who thought that poetry was entirely image. I read a very early book by C. Day Lewis in which he argued that poetry is metaphor and nothing else (though you wouldn't know it from his practice), and that view is still something of a dogma in America. Right now so much of the young American poetry seems to be enormously influenced by Robert Bly. I think Bly was a very fresh and vital influence at first, but now I see so many young poets publishing books of Bly-influenced surrealistic imagery and little else. Like Sylvia Plath, Bly has had an influence that has been the origin of an awful lot of bad poetry.

Do you feel that too many contemporary poets are given to exploiting their personalities, and do you regret poems based on such an egoism?

I'm slightly bored with poets' personalities. Berryman is an exception in that he has an interesting personality. Quite frankly I get bored by, let's say, Anne Sexton's personality, though she was far from untalented, but she might have written better if she'd chosen to write a different kind of poem.

Perhaps with more sense of formalism?

Yes, and thus she would have got more into her subject matter which would have been the world rather than herself. I remember one of her poems which treats a visit to the dentist as a major tragedy.

You wrote some time ago that poets who write in very controlled forms often have a strong sense of personal anarchy about them. Is that something you've felt about yourself?

Experience is unstructured, but once you start writing a poem it becomes subject to certain limits—metre, rhyme, or the fluid rhythms of free verse. Shakespeare was writing within colossal limits, for an extraordinarily crude stage compared with the modern stage. The limits can be quite narrow and still have interesting results, they help define the thing itself.

Your view is continuous, I suppose, with Yvor Winters's opinion that the poem creates a meaning and also evaluates the experience: one defines the experience and educes an idea about it, in order to understand it.

I would prefer to use not the word evaluation but another phrase he uses, the attempt to understand. It sounds less final. The attempt to understand is also part of the experience of the poem, whereas evaluation does sound a little bit like marking a student's paper.

You wrote a marvellous lecture on Hardy in 1970 in which you show how the ballad and the reflective lyric are closely aligned. But at one point you also say that it's very difficult for a modern poet to leave out a social context in writing a poem. Were you implying that it's necessary for the poet to get away from the immediacy of his environment?

I don't remember the passage, but I certainly *wouldn't* say it's necessary. The process of becoming a better artist lies in opening up more and more areas that you can speak about. One of the limitations of my first books is that I had been reading so much Shakespeare, Donne and Stendhal, and I was writing about the heroic. I wasn't able to bring in too much of my experience because so little of it fitted in with this vague idea of the heroic. I remember G. S. Fraser, in an otherwise very nice review, said that one thing Thom Gunn lacks is a sense of humour, and indeed I wasn't able to bring humour into poems until quite a bit later. The breakthroughs in my poetry have all been into new areas, new kinds of experience.

Would you censure your first couple of volumes for being a bit too water-tight, too hermetic?

I don't regret them. I just think they were limited as many people's early books are limited, both in subject matter and style.

There is possibly too much intellectual control about them, too much wariness about leaving yourself open?

That could be, though I'd say it more of the second book than of the first.

The thematic unity of the first book hinges to a great extent on an idea of a clash, a conflict, a dialogue, between self-consciousness and control, doesn't it? In the first poem, 'The Wound', the wound itself would be the instinctual life controlled by social form.

Yes. That's very well put. I think that 'The Wound' is my first real poem.

And in several poems such as 'Wind in the Street' or 'Helen's Rape' you have the opposition between 'forced content' and 'the violent dreamed escape'. In a sense it seems that the first two books pursue a kind of dialectic which is synthesized in the third book where you accept the need for urgency, determination, and will . . .

I'm happier living with them in that book.

And perhaps your most gentle book of all is Touch.

Yes. I was trying to reach forward into something new. I think the end of the first phase is the first half of *My Sad Captains*, and the beginning of the second phase is the syllabic poems in the second half of that book. *Touch* took a long time to write, partly because I didn't yet know fully what I was trying to reach towards.

In a sense the first two books are bubbling with a kind of frustration, aren't they?

I think so, yes, and almost irritability. That dreadful, silly, bad poem 'Lines for a Book', which has become notorious, is a very naked example of that. It's one of the few poems I'd really want to exclude.

Fighting Terms *presents a kind of brief for excess as opposed to the cautious sapience we all go in for, and it's paradoxical that in the first two books you're trying to force the issues and break certain barriers. In 'A Kind of Ethics', for example, you enunciate a position of some extremism.*

The most thoroughgoing of those poems is 'Incident on a Journey', where I say 'when a living impulse came/I acted, and my impulse made me wise', and that's pure romantic doctrine, isn't it?

In 'Carnal Knowledge' you take up the aspect of one's pose in life; in that poem it's the pose lovers assume towards one another. You treat the fact of separateness between two people in the sense that we may share our bodies but we are always distinct persons underneath . . .

Yes, and of course by the time I come to 'Touch' I'm saying just the opposite. It's a question of growing up.

Yes, I wanted to mention that, because I'd noticed the contradiction in the point of view.

It's a complete reversal, really.

Well, reversal, yes, and yet even in the earlier poems you have an implied sense of envy of natural life, of the energy and unself-consciousness of animals, for example.

I think that's still in my poetry. I think many human beings have an envy for the simple, instinctual life, but the great paradox is that this envy is expressed through words and the intelligence and couldn't be expressed in any other way. We wouldn't have the envy if we didn't have words and minds, and it's paradoxical that our ability to express it can be superior to the instinctual life.

In The Sense of Movement *you are extremely forceful about the elements of risk and danger we must face in life. But then I feel your poem 'Elvis Presley' is ambivalent in that you're celebrating his pose, if you like, and at the same time registering a sense of pathos about those who live vicariously, who can't even begin to emulate Presley's style of revolt.*

Most of my poems are ambivalent. I don't remember that poem too clearly, but what I think I'm expressing is that art is one of the ways in which we can overcome the inadequacies of the condition we find ourselves living in, and as such it's a very Paterian kind of attitude. I don't find it a very good poem; there are phrases I like, but it's awfully journalistic, superficial. It's one of my poems that became well known because of its subject matter.

If we take it that many of the early poems are inviting the reader to court violence or extremism, did you feel then and do you perhaps still feel somewhat pedagogic in your work?

I suppose I am, yes. A friend of mine remarked last year that all my poems are didactic, which struck me all of a heap. Perhaps there is more of the pedagogue in me than in someone like Ted Hughes, or the early Gary Snyder, though he's become almost exclusively pedagogic since about 1970. I'm trying to explain values to myself, and since I have readers I'm not just doing it for myself. But I'm not sure how different I am from many other poets in doing that.

But I have a strong sense that you were exhorting the reader . . .

Well, yes, especially in the first two volumes.

Following up what we were saying about man's envy for natural instinctual life, your poem called 'The Unsettled Motorcyclist's Vision of his Death' also explores the irony of the fact that, although we envy spontaneous energy, nature lacks man's capacity for decision and will; non-human life cannot decide for danger.

As I remember it in that poem it becomes a distaste for nature, or horror of it. The motorcyclist thought he was so secure on his machine—man-made, self-created—but once he becomes part of nature he gets taken over and swallowed in roots. It's an emotional situation, not a didactic one. *I*'ve never thought of myself as a didactic poet.

Among the poems I like very much from your second book is 'Autumn Chapter in a Novel'.

Yes, even then I admired the kind of poem where meaning is achieved through the images, through a description—something which could be reducible to a statement but the statement isn't made anywhere. A poem I've loved since I first read it is Williams's 'Spring and All', and what's so terrific is the way it simply consists of description, and yet it is making statements about what it is like to be born.

To take just one further poem from The Sense of Movement, *I imagine that you still feel sympathetic to the poem called 'A Plan of Self Subjection'—'tracing circles is a useful spell/Against contentment'—in that the idea of the poem concerns restlessness and enquiry . . .*

I would still say something like that, yes. I saw contentment as a kind of sloth. I think it's a great danger for poets and artists to get too satisfied with what they're doing. I think particularly of Gary Snyder, whom I wrote about on a couple of occasions prior to 1970, and I still think that his poetry of the 1950s and 1960s is magnificent. Since 1970 he's published two books, and I've seen various other poems of his, but there are only a couple of poems that I like. I certainly wouldn't venture to say he is self-satisfied. He's leading the kind of life he intended to lead, he has disciples living on his ranch, he seems to be extremely happy, and he's writing what he ought to write—pious ecology and pious Buddhism—but there's no restlessness in the poetry and it's gone very flat.

Touch *seems to resolve the issues, or at least the angle, of your first books by approaching the subjects in a more humane way . . .*

Yes, that was the way out—to be more humane.

. . . and there is something assertive about the first two volumes which you moderated by the third.

Awfully assertive. I'm immediately limiting the heroic at the end of the first poem in *My Sad Captains*, 'In Santa Maria del Popolo', which is about a picture of St. Paul but which also takes notice of the poor old women praying in the chapel. So that to some extent I've gone out into the world, away from the first two books and the blustering heroism of people who are self-regarding. I praised and exalted such people as if there were no other way of getting outside oneself, and that was the limitation of the first two books. Getting outside oneself was one of the things I learned from Williams, who's been very important to me for a long time. I knew I had a lot to learn.

But you didn't submerge the concerns you'd shown in your earlier work.

No, I wasn't going to submit to anything.

The impetus remained perhaps similar, but you seemed to become less categorical.

I should also say that it's not just a matter of ideas, but of a development in the way I treated the ideas, which involves all the possible stylistic considerations including the rhythmical. In a sense, as soon as I moved away from metre into a more improvisational mode—that is, syllabics—I got into a more generous frame of writing. I found room for the more unexpected life, the unexpected emotion, maybe for greater sympathy. That may not be true of free verse as a whole, but of my use of syllabics in that particular book.

In the poem called 'Hotblood on Friday' you extol a richness of experience and seem to point to the limitations of consciousness or rationality. It sounds as if there was possibly an anti-intellectual drift in your work at that stage.

It's too easy, as it were, to be anti-intellectual. I respect the intellect too much. No, I'm doing there what I'm always trying to do—to have my cake and eat it. I think I've been trying to do that from the beginning, to have as much of the instinctual life as possible but also as much of the intelligent life as possible.

... which is presumably why you use a phrase like 'limiting candor' in 'Flying above California': we must be honest with our intelligence and recognize that we can never become quite like non-human life. In the first of the two poems called 'Modes of Pleasure' you seem to say that we must exercise our intelligence and not accede to habits of being which stultify.

Yes. It's a very Baudelairean poem, I think, though not consciously. I've always admired Baudelaire a lot.

Your emphasis so far has understandably been on ideas, but I certainly don't see myself as a philosopher or even as that consistent a thinker. For me poems are experiences, and the ideas in them are always modified by the language, by the rhythms, by the form of the poem. So I should make that proviso when we're speaking about ideas. I have seldom considered them as abstractly as you do. I think much more consciously of the subject matter initiating a poem, and since I hold certain general ideas at a certain time about human behaviour my choice of subject matter and my treatment of it are going to be influenced by such ideas, maybe permeated by such ideas, quite often not consciously. And I'd say the later you get in my poetry the less consciously do I speculate about ideas while I'm writing the poem. Writing a poem is sometimes just a way of dealing with things in my life. Poetry has become much more a part of my way of living in the last fifteen years than it was in the first fifteen years of my career.

Yet one of the things for which you've been most praised is your ability to use ideas in verse, while so many poets seem unversed in anything other than techniques of metaphor and image-making.

I think of myself as a writer about experience modified by ideas; those ideas in turn are modified by experience, and so on endlessly.

The poem is a process much more than any sort of pre-formulation?

Certainly. A poem is obviously an artifact, but it's also part of my experience of living. Poetry is an action, one of many different kinds of action such as taking a walk, eating a meal, or making love. When I first started writing I would have emphasized the view of poem as artifact.

I suppose I've drawn certain conclusions from some of your early essays in which you stressed the conscious, willed aspects of writing a poem, and seemed to foreclose the possibilities of serendipity.

Yes, and my earlier poetry invites that emphasis also. There have been some articles about me which have been solely concerned with my ideas, almost as if I were a lay philosopher.

You've said that your earlier work was influenced by Sartre, but there's much more of Camus behind Touch, *isn't there?*

Oh yes. There's a lot of Camus behind 'Misanthropos', the long poem. It's a pervading feeling; I don't know if it comes in specific parts, maybe in the action after the other people turn up, when the man finds that he isn't alone. I was re-reading Camus in the early 1960s when I wrote the poem.

'Misanthropos' came to be a long poem by stages, didn't it? It was your first venture into writing a long poem.

Well, I've only had two ventures, the other poem being 'Jack Straw's Castle'.

What about 'Geysers'?

Well, that's a poem joined together by theme rather than by narrative, but I know what you mean. I began writing 'Misanthropos' with what became one of the later sections—XIV—in which a man who has survived a catastrophic war sees other people approaching him; but I got stuck for the simple reason that I had far too much exposition to get into the poem, so it went unfinished for a while. Then I had hepatitis and spent almost two months in bed, and by the end of that time I conceived of this as one of a group of pastoral poems, using some pastoral forms from the Elizabethans—an echo poem, for example—and another where I use the form of one of Marvell's Mower poems—alternating pentameter and tetrameter lines rhyming in couplets—'Elegy on the Dust'. So at that stage I saw it as being a group of loosely related pastoral poems, and then later it became the story that had been implicit from the start. I realized that I had a lot more things I wanted to talk about by way of the experience of the hero.

One of the stages he goes through, of course, is a sense of resistance, where he is jealous of his isolation. In reaching other people he learns to extend himself but the irony is that in being named by them he also has to limit himself.

Yes. The influence of Camus, now I think of it, came from his last novel, *La Chute*, which was on my mind in the section called 'Memoirs of the World', where the hero looks back on his past, just as the hero in *La Chute* is constantly looking back. I think it's

Camus's best single work of art. I was also reading a lot of Thomas Mann at the time, and there is a little novel called *The Holy Sinner* where a hermit becomes animal-like. I took a lot of hints from there.

A number of critics have not particularly liked the poem, it may be because it strikes them as a little laboured, though it does seem to me that the tentativeness of your exploration is right for the poem.

That's certainly what I was aiming at, a tentativeness to each section.

Can you say something about the poem called 'Innocence', which is perfect in the way it controls what is actually an horrific incident?

It's a little too perfect in a way, a little too polished. I got the incident itself from a book called *Autobiography of an SS Man*, translated by Constantine FitzGibbon, which showed how somebody who began as a humane person could commit an atrocity. I dedicated it to Tony White, one of my best friends, since we had discussed this kind of thing. I was visiting Berlin at the time I wrote it, in about 1960. One had derived a very melodramatic view of Germany from reading newspapers during the war, and one hadn't speculated much on what it might be like for an ordinary German soldier—not a monster—drawn into monstrous situations. I find the poem now a little too clear and polished.

In Touch *as a whole you set a premium on the full sensory life.*

Yes, right. It's what happens at the end of 'Misanthropos'—the actual physical touch. 'Confessions of a Life Artist' in that book is perhaps one of the last of my self-consciousness poems. The man is a Life Artist in that he thinks he can control his life like a work of art. He's not me, he's somebody who's got fucked up by his consciousness. Everything is rather too perfectly as he'd intended it to be, but at the same time he's missed out. I suppose, now I think about it, it's a little like Henry James's 'The Beast in the Jungle', a story I just read again recently: I was aiming for something like that. At the end he realizes that what he's missed is nothing tangible. In a sense that fictional character is one side of any human being. As a pimp he possesses all these beautiful girls, he possesses them but he can never be them.

Touch is a weird book for me, I still don't know whether some of the poems come off: 'Back to Life' is one such. I know what I wanted to do in the poem, but I don't know whether my will is manipulating things a little too much, or whether it's fully there as an experience. I hope it is, but I don't know. In that poem and 'The Produce District' I used what I've called to myself the Lycidas form, by which I mean that most of the lines rhyme but are of different lengths. I feel much more secure about 'Pierce Street'.

'In the Tank' presumably derives something from Camus when you use the image of the figure being suspended in a box?

It's also one of my most nightmarish feelings, not just an appropriate philosophical image. I remember once hearing an awful story about someone who decided to commit suicide by locking himself inside a huge refrigerator, and that method of suicide by suffocation strikes me as very terrifying.

You've written that you're eternally grateful for not having been brought up with any religion.

Well, many of my friends have been Catholics, and it may be that Catholic education in America is or has been rather rigid and barbarous. I find that ex-Catholics have far more feeling against their religion than those who have given up other faiths. I'm just glad I didn't have that additional confusion on top of all my other confusions when I was growing up. I suppose that makes me rather an unspiritual person. I'm not a dogmatic materialist, I'm aware that there are many possible communications in existence that I don't know about. In fact it often strikes me that just as animals are colour-blind we may be blind to other senses. I'm just grateful that I wasn't brought up with any dogma. It does seem possible that there might be some kind of life after death. James Merrill's recent work, which is about séances, is extraordinarily interesting. Merrill says quite honestly that he doesn't know whether it's all self-projection, but even if it's complete delusion *Mirabel* is still a wonderful book to read.

Could you say something about your intentions in writing Moly*?*

The thing is that looked at from one point of view the book is largely about LSD, but I didn't want to limit it to an audience who had experience of drugs. It's my favourite book by myself, partly because it's the neglected child. I also think that I extended my range a great deal in the poetry of the book, and I'm not sure I've got very far beyond it yet. It's a phase of my writing life that I'm probably still in—not that it is only about drugs. Poems like 'From the Wave' were in some way answering an earlier poem like 'On the Move', and I hope a poem like 'Being Born' can be understood purely in metaphorical terms. The theme of the book as a whole, if you like to speak in those terms, is of metamorphosis, as in the second poem where the man is actually being turned into a pig. Taking LSD and writing *Moly* was an answer to the tentativeness of *Touch.*

Can you elaborate a little on how LSD gave you access to new experience?

You get a new sense of possibilities. That's the tremendous thing it did for me. My friends and I began to discover new possibilities in practical terms in our lives that we hadn't paid too much attention to since our early twenties. I'm not speaking of the immediate effect of taking the drug, but the after-effect: it was an opening instead of a closing down. It was in 1966 that I gave up my regular job of teaching, not by coincidence. They had in fact been very nice to me and promoted me to such an extent that I was spending too much time on administrative work, and I found no time to write a poem. I still teach part-time—for Berkeley—but just one term a year. It's not highly-paid, and in fact I have the lowest rank, but it's an ideal situation for me.

Moly *seems to show a hankering for some way to harmonize the passional life with the mental life, it's not an abnegation.*

In this case of course the working of the mind was often through metre. It became a conscious choice for the book to be in metre, since I wrote a number of the poems in metre before I realized what I was doing, and I continued to do so when I did realize it.

The general posture of the book is that it is nourishing to put oneself in contact with the rhythms of nature, Antaeus-like.

Yes. That's another reason why I like the book, since I was able to bring myself to an acceptance that I hadn't managed in previous books. I was trying to do that kind of thing in *Touch*, but I don't think I entirely succeeded except in the poem called 'Touch'.

Yet the paradox of 'Composing uncomposed' (a phrase from the last line of 'Words') remains, doesn't it, since you're immersing yourself in new feelings and rhythms and yet having to detach yourself for the task of composition?

Exactly. 'Composing uncomposed' is in a sense not having your cake and not eating it.

Don't you have some sort of quarrel in the book with too much cerebral life, the limitations of consciousness?

Well, I don't think I explicitly come up against it.

Perhaps in 'Flooded Meadows'?

No, I'd think the opposite. I think I'm being 'intellectual' there, as you'd say.

> Yet definition is suspended, for,
> In pools across the level listlessness,
> Light answers only light before the breeze,
> Cancelling the rutted, weedy, slow brown floor
> For the unity of unabsorbed excess.

The light is solipsistic in a sense, and cancels all the accretions of experience, simplifying it into maybe one marvellous LSD trance where the real world has been glamorized as pure abstract light. It's cancelled for a unity of ambiguous value, perhaps the unity of the moron—'the unity of unabsorbed excess'—and I'm not using the word 'excess' in the sense Blake used it. So that's the intellect bringing back control at that point.

I suppose I'd infer from the book as a whole that you regret the way in which we generally apprehend the world, which is to say that we expropriate an idea from life and so limit it.

Yes, that would be a general tenor.

It may be that some critics have reservations about the book because it seems to give credence to more of a mindless absorption in experience.

Surely that's what most conventional critics might actually applaud—a romanticism which does not introduce the intellect. Some critics have a tremendously sentimental delight in the poetry of sheer passion. I don't read all the critics say about me, though I have read Clive Wilmer's article . . .[1]

Yes, that must be the best and most heartening article ever written about you.

. . . and a wonderful piece about *Jack Straw's Castle* by Colin Falck which was very sympathetic and helpful.[2] But in my experience a lot of critics are scared of being too intellectual or cerebral. What was reassuring to me was that of the reviewers I read on *Moly* most disliked it for different reasons.

Although critics should perhaps like the book because it's dealing with things which are quite other than abstract, I suppose that many people would feel threatened by it.

To do them justice, they may have felt that I was being too modish. I was certainly taking up something at the fashionable time.

Positives *seems to me very reminiscent of William Carlos Williams.*

Yes, I was quite conscious of that. Talbot Road, the block in which I lived for a year, is shown in the picture on the back cover, though it's all been pulled down now. When I came back to London that year I found that my brother had developed into a very good photographer and he'd in fact already taken some of the pictures we used in the book, such as the girl on the dodgems who is dancing to herself and had no idea my brother was taking the picture. We often went out together when he took pictures, so the book defined itself as we went along. I planned the poems mostly as versified captions, though I think a few do come off as poems. I didn't have high ambitions about them. Doing the book certainly helped me to get to the stage of *Moly*, though in a way it would be difficult to trace.

A fair part of your next book, Jack Straw's Castle, *is based on reminiscence.*

Yes, and maybe it's because of age. I'd perhaps reached an age when I was thinking more objectively about my childhood than I had been able to do before.

[1] Definition and Flow: A Personal Reading of Thom Gunn', *PN Review*, vol. 5 no. 3, 1978, pp. 51–7.

[2] 'Uncertain Violence', *New Review*, vol. 3 no. 32, November 1976, pp. 37–41.

'Geysers' seems to be the ultimate stage of surrendering yourself to a total body experience . . . camping out, the waters . . .

Also I was trying to write different kinds of couplets; each section is in couplets.

Isn't there a danger that 'The Geysers' expresses so much personal exultation that it's become almost a private poem, as at the end:

> *torn from the self*
> *in which I breathed and trod*
> *I am*
> *I am raw meat*
> *I am a god*

The fictional 'I' was becoming an Orpheus there, torn to pieces by the Thracian women. The question is whether I've made the experience come to life in the style, and I'm not sure about that poem. Maybe it's one of those poems that's good in performance but doesn't hold up when you read it. There was originally another section which I published in a pamphlet, but it struck me as too didactic.

Are you aware or even wary of the fact that the book commits itself so strongly to a full sensory life that it might seem to disavow our self-consciousness?

I don't think so much of its effect on the reader as its truth to myself. I think my mind is looking after itself pretty well, and I can give myself up as much as possible to the sensory life at the same time. I don't feel any threat to what's going on in my mind, which keeps working. It may sound a boastful thing to say, but I think that's so.

You don't wish 'The Geysers' to be taken as a credo or even as a manifesto for the good life?

It's *a* life. I'm not claiming more than that.

In 'The Outdoor Concert' you say that 'At the edge/of the understanding:/it's the secret', which must be taken as an assertion.

It certainly is. I'm maybe trying to direct the reader back to his own experience with music. I've realized since I wrote the poem that there's a huge borrowing from what Margaret Schlegel says about music in *Howard's End*, though I'm not sure she uses the word 'secret'. (I don't mind acknowledging my debts since one of the sources of literature is literature, poetry derives from poetry.) The poem is about The Grateful Dead, not Beethoven.

Could you construe the poem called 'Dolly' a little?

Well, I'm saying that the self-destructive welcome symbols of self-destruction, though they may not know what they are. It's all there on the surface of the poem, and in fact I've tried to get simpler in my work in general. I mean, 'A Mirror for Poets' (in my first book, *Fighting Terms*) contains a reference to the Paphlagonian King, which is taken from Sidney's *Arcadia*. It's an almost unforgivably obscure reference, but I thought at the time that you have to do that in poetry.

I think I would like to be understood more easily now, which doesn't mean less complexity in the subject matter but it means bringing it up to the surface. I think the best poem in *Jack Straw's Castle* is 'The Idea of Trust', since it can be readily understood but the implications are complicated. I like a simple poem to imply a lot of other things besides itself. The one obscure reference in 'Jack Straw's Castle' is 'Little Ease', which is from Fulke Greville, as I explained in the introduction to my selection from his work (where I associate the phrase with Camus). But readers would also find it in the *OED*. There *are* other references—to Dante, for example—which it doesn't matter so much if readers understand, and there's even a reference to Robert Louis Stevenson's *Kidnapped*, where his wicked uncle sends him up some stone stairs at night without a candle. If somebody recognizes those references, it's great, but they're not the substance of the poem.

Would you acknowledge that there may be something wilful about the resolution of the poem?

> *The beauty's in what is, not what may seem.*
> *I turn. And even if he were a dream*
> *—Thick sweating flesh against which I lie curled—*
> *With dreams like this, Jack's ready for the world.*

Well, the point is that Jack is speaking about himself in the third person, and when do people do that?—when they're not very sure of themselves. Richard III says 'Richard's himself again.' There's a certain bravado in that last section, since he's uttering conditional clauses: there's no certainty that he won't have to make the nightmare journey again. Part 2 is actually a transcription of something I heard through my bathroom window:

> Pig pig she cries
> I can hear her from next door
> He fucked me in the mouth
> And now he won't give me car fare
> she rages and cries

—which is about as opposed as two bodies could be, and the end of the poem is at least an elementary answer to that, a return to touch. So I don't think the end is wilful, I felt I'd worked my way through to it.

Can you say what other features of the book you think peculiar to it or important to you?

I think there's a lot of uneasiness in the book. It's interesting that you should have spoken of the good life earlier: there's a great line from a song by The Grateful Dead—'Having a hard time living the good life'—and that could be an epigraph to *Jack Straw's Castle.* If it advocates anything it's not something easy ... maybe in 'The Geysers', but not elsewhere. There's 'The Corporal', which is about death, or there's the uneasiness behind the poem about horse chestnut trees as to whether it's possible to remember the past with any accuracy, and there's 'Jack Straw's Castle', where if the return is to the good life there's been so much nightmare preceding it that the good life is only on the surface. Even in 'The Geysers' the third part—about the geyser itself—is not happy. Parts 1 and 2, although pretty joyful, have to be taken together with the third part, which undercuts them completely. The fourth part itself is a fantasy, but the fantasy of Orpheus is one in which you pay for the sensual life by having your body torn to pieces.

So that in fact very little of the book at all is really postulated on the view that we can find fulfilment by breaking the bonds of consciousness and civility?

I'd say that breaking the bonds is something we can try for, but probably not succeed in doing. During the most exalted days of taking LSD I remember thinking that it's different from Christian's experience in *Pilgrim's Progress* in that while Christian drops his burden of sin I think we don't drop our burden; I don't call it sin, I just call it past experience. You carry the burden of everything you know on your back: it's a very interesting burden, I don't regret it, I like it. I don't want to drop it into the river that comes before the Heavenly City.

It's not Camus's burden of guilt?

No, it's not the same. It's all past experience, sensual joys, mistakes, everything. I think that just as in 'The Idea of Trust'—as somebody pointed out to me last night—it could be seen that I understand the character Jim's predicament so well that I sympathize with him. And that's how I'd like the whole book to be taken, as facing both ways. What I want to get across is that one can learn from the ecstasy just as well as one can learn from the mistakes and unhappiness. They modify each other.

I like the economy and the attention to the object of a poem like 'Hampstead: the Horse Chestnut Trees', but do you feel there may be an element of over-elaboration in 'Jack Straw's Castle' and 'The Geysers', as though you were forcing the issue?

I know what you're saying, though I don't agree with it.

Unlike some critics I do like the humour you've got into the book in poems such as 'Courage, a Tale', which some reviewers criticized as bathetic, the wrong sort of whimsy.

It's just a joke, and it's meant to be tasteless. The poem called 'Yoko' is about a colossal Newfoundland dog owned by a friend of mine in New York. I wanted to write a poem that is completely doggy, since so many poems about animals—by Lawrence, Marianne Moore, or Ted Hughes—are marvellous, but the subjects are dealt with from a human point of view. There's a wonderful line in Hughes's 'Pike'—'stunned by their own grandeur'—but it's not really true. I don't criticize that kind of poem for a moment, but I wanted to write a poem that is all dog. Then I read Gertrude Stein's *Three Lives* and I found the enthusiastic but naïve voice I could use, and I was delighted that I could even find a Jamesian phrase at one point when the dog is sniffing a turd—'I can place it finely'—but of course James was one of Gertrude Stein's masters. Once I'd got the key, I enjoyed writing the poem.

And you're touching sentimentality of course.

I don't see anything wrong with writing about sentiment as such, not wallowing in it as we normally mean by the word sentimentality. In Leavis's Cambridge sentimentality was one of the great awful words, but if you're not going to write about sentiment you're cutting out a large part of human experience. But it is tricky. A greater danger of sentimentality might be in 'The Cherry Tree', but I like that poem too. On the other hand I feel a poem like 'Behind the Mirror' is a rather scrappy poem, though the ideas are sound enough. I think it's a little incomplete, since the two sections are separate, not joined together. The reader has to make the leap, I don't make it. The theme is more conventionally serious there, but the execution is not as adventurous as it is in 'Yoko' or 'The Cherry Tree'.

Do you feel you've been less polemical in recent verse?

There may be polemicism in 'Touch', but I don't think I'm so different from any other poet in that direction. I write from imagination and experience, and don't think of myself as a poet of ideas in the way that Jonson or Shelley or Fulke Greville were.

In a poem such as 'The Release' you show a tremendous respect for the integrity of the lives of other people; you don't commandeer their experience for the sake of your subjective views but acknowledge their independence.

Yes, I'm *not* saying I could encapsulate the experience of others.

Can you tell me about your work in progress?

I have about twenty-four poems, but I don't see a pattern for my next book yet. I feel peculiarly inadequate in speaking about work in progress. There seems to be a unity to one's interests that one's not very conscious of, and it becomes apparent only after a while, at which stage I realize that I've got a book. *Moly* is only twenty-five poems, because I realized the pattern earlier.

Do you feel you can claim kin with certain other poets? I mean, for so long you were yoked together with Ted Hughes . . .

Yes, and we have almost nothing in common. I find myself

working on my own. I was reading a book of short stories by Scott Fitzgerald the other day—*Taps at Reveille*—and I realized that he and I have something like the same strategies in common. He's a big old romantic, and you can tell from his first books just how awful and slushy that romanticism could be, but then he suddenly became more artistic and aware. Like Stendhal, as he gets older he gets more intelligent, but his intelligence doesn't destroy the romantic figures, it abets them, it helps them to come alive. In *La Chartreuse de Parme*, Fabrice is something like a Sabatini here, but his charming blunders and misconceptions don't invalidate him—on the contrary it is they that enable us to believe in his good-hearted bravery. Fitzgerald's terrific in describing these wonderful girls and they come to life in a way that you can't deny them, but he's retaining his irony and criticism. The irony, as with Stendhal, doesn't undercut the romanticism, it actually reinforces it, and I think this is what I've been doing throughout. I've had my romantic notions, which have varied somewhat, but I've been trying to make them intelligible and to bring them to life other than by simply celebrating them in a kind of dumb way. I am romantic, and I try to make the objects of my romanticism credible. It's romantic subject matter rather than romantic techniques. I'm trying to make what might often seem to be untenable emotions or unadmirable subjects—feelings which I find attractive—credible. In a poem such as 'On the Move' I'm treating a subject which at that time I found heroic in my own terms, since that kind of heroism is my early subject. That's the way I see myself as Fitzgerald, so there's a kinship. I learned an awful lot from associating as a friend with Robert Duncan, who taught me a great deal without knowing it.

But in answer to your question, no, I don't know anybody who's trying to do the kind of thing I'm trying to do most of the time.

You presumably can't say whether you think of yourself as an English poet?

It's a question of almost unbelievable difficulty. Donald Davie's review of my *Selected Poems* [*New Republic* 13 October 1979] seems to me the only statement that has made any plausible distinction between what American poetry is now and what English poetry is, and I think he says very well in what ways I'm English and American. It's a lovely review, too.

Do you think you'll continue to live in America?

I think I'm quite committed to it. I'm much less well known as a poet in America, but I'm scared of too much applause, and I don't need the company of other poets. My friends are not particularly literary, they tend to be plumbers or carpenters. California has become the most populated state in the Union since I've been living there, so most of the people I know come from different parts of America. I have a weird feeling in London that I'm an American tourist and yet I know it all. I possess two lives but not lives that are opposed. I certainly feel that English and American literature are two different entities, but for me they're all one thing. Shakespeare and Wallace Stevens are united in my experience of them, and so are Dante and Baudelaire. Consequently I don't feel I need to answer to myself the question of whether I'm part of an American or an English tradition.

SEAMUS HEANEY

How do you approach the writing of each poem: do you hold them for hours or days, perhaps even months?

It varies. I tended, in the beginning, to move fast at it, and that was part of the excitement. Then you begin to get to know your proper subjects and you tend to go slower and relish the thing. When I read, for example, *The Bog People*, about the Tollund Man, I knew I'd write a poem about it. But I was very, very timorous of starting.

Was it the text or the photographs which spurred you?

I think it was the photographs really ... I've been thinking about that man ever since: that fascination with him overcomes almost everybody who looks at him. He looks like an ancestor; he looks like every photograph of a great uncle in every house in Europe. He's slightly archaic, but not 'other'. It's partly that it's a human head with the status of a work of art. Very strange, but it's very familiar, that face, I've seen it in coffins so often in my adolescence. I used to go to a lot of funerals and to wakes, kneeling beside the coffins at eye level with aged *rigor mortis* heads. I knew I would write about it, but I was timorous in case I would make a balls of it.

There's another little poem which is in the new book, it's nothing particular to look at or notice but its gestation was interesting too. One evening, I went fishing with a friend of mine called Barrie Cook, tench fishing. They're a toothless fish and they send up bubbles—they love the slime and the mud, and you fish for them in the dark. There's this kind of slimy goodness about them; they told me they were called a doctor fish because there was a superstition that the slime upon them healed wounded fish—pike and so on—that touched them as they went past. Then later on I was in a hotel up around County Monaghan one night, feeling strange and poetically barren, and there was a dance on, a lot of country kids listening to pop music, and at about half past one they came out over the car park, and these absolute dialect voices came bubbling up to me. It was like a vision of the kind of life I had in the fifties, going to dances and so on, and I felt the redemptive quality of the dialect, of the guttural, the illiterate self.

What you call in one poem, 'our guttural muse'.

Yes. In fact I called this poem 'The Guttural Muse' when I eventually wrote it. I held those two things in my head for two years, and then suddenly I wrote it down. But maybe I let them lie too long, because those original elements didn't generate anything more out of themselves in the end.

Do most poems need that sort of impulse, a prompting . . .

Oh yes.

. . . rather than simply a mood?

You often have the mood with nothing to do with it, and I'm never sure what is the proper way to proceed then.

Is it a matter of keeping your senses open?

Yes, and actually I think that's why poets shouldn't work too hard at other jobs, because I think if you commit a lot of your attention and your tension in another place, you close those receiving stations. I think that if you're going to be a poet, you have to think of yourself as a poet. This doesn't mean behaving like a literary person or anything; it is a vocation, an inward preserving of a stance or an attitude or a readiness. And I think you can sin against your own gift by not remembering always to keep it ready; and you can sin against it by being moral in another way, you know, looking after a job. Like Matthew Arnold—stunned by morality.

Do you find being back at teaching now discharges that sort of mood, defuses it in a way?

Not the teaching . . . I don't actually mind the activity, I quite like it, and one great thing about this teaching I'm doing—the terrific redemptive thing—is that I really believe in it. I resigned from teaching in Queen's University in 1972 and I was out in Wicklow for four years, and when I came back to teaching, I came back with great ease, and with very . . . not low aims, but I think real aims. It's a teacher's training college, and I said to myself, if I can get these girls to read about twelve to twenty poems a year, over three years they may know within themselves about thirty or forty poems. That seems to me to be quite a large achievement. I love them to read poems and I love to read poems to them. I suppose I'm a bit of a bully about the thing.

When you were in Wicklow, you were working on a Middle Irish romance, which gave you a discipline for writing every day. Did you come away from that situation because you felt you weren't getting enough out of it?

It certainly wasn't because I didn't feel I was getting enough out of the situation. Spiritually I felt terrifically steadied. The circumstances of life were difficult, especially as we lived at a good distance from the main road. The house was small and it wasn't our own. We had come to Wicklow in transition and ended up almost staying. But there were always thoughts of children's schooling. I foresaw that if we stayed in Wicklow, in Glanmore, about twenty-five or thirty miles south of Dublin, I foresaw the teenage years of the children as being slightly disconsolate, running into Dublin, and all that; and I saw a repetition of the kind of thing I used to go through when I was in my teens in County Derry, fights about the car . . . who'll get the car . . . I suppose that for the first time in my life, I thought of the future, and in order to set the domestic machinery quietly and efficiently to work, I thought we'd move into Dublin.

I didn't actually want to go back to the university, strangely enough, because the kind of figure you cut within the community of the university is a public one, I think, and what I dearly wanted at that time was a private beat. I have this feeling that in a college of education it's a much quieter, lower profile, and the teaching suits me better. I like nesting and I like giving out what I believe, and saying the same things over again. And also I believe that student teachers—who are going to be primary teachers—are the most important body. So much in

Ireland still needs to be done . . . the definition of the culture, and the redefinition of it. If you could open the students into trust in their own personality, into some kind of freedom and cultivation, you could do a hell of a lot.

Now, it's a Catholic college you teach at . . . has the Faith been a solid ground with you all your life?

I'm not what you'd call a pious Catholic, I don't go to Mass much, and the doctrines of the Faith aren't my constant reading . . . but, I guess it was part of the texture of growing up. I was going to Confession into my twenties, and the whole of my life was permeated with it. I've never felt any need to rebel or do a casting-off of God or anything like that, because I think in this day anthropologists and mythologists have taught us a lot, to live with our myths.

You don't find their procedures militate against what we call a creed?

I don't probe too far . . .

In the sense that you're not theoretical about it; you're more concerned with what Yeats called 'making a soul'?

That area of thinking is something that's only come to me recently. I think the power of the Church as a political force is much less . . . but the point is, the people want it. The country's made up of solid burghers who believe in these probities. There's a tremendous complacency in the Irish Catholic middle class, which has to do with going to Mass, among other things. Everything in this country is bathed in it. I don't think it's much to do with Christianity; Irish Catholicism is continuous with something older than Christianity. In fact, Christianity is about the best thing you could have if you could actually go through with it!

My sensibility was formed by the dolorous murmurings of the rosary, and the generally Marian quality of devotion. The reality that was addressed was maternal, and the posture was one of supplication. The attitude to life that was inculcated into me—not by priests, but by the active, lived thing of prayers and so on, in my house, through my mother—was really patience. At the bottom I think that probably patience is the best virtue. Irish Catholicism, until about ten years ago, had this Virgin Mary worship, almost worship. In practice, the shrines, the rosary beads, all the devotions, were centred towards a feminine presence, which I think was terrific for the sensibility. I think that the 'Hail Mary' is more of a poem than the 'Our Father'. 'Our Father' is between chaps, but there's something faintly amorous about the 'Hail Mary'.

Why is the maternal aspect so pre-eminent for you?

There's a kind of voice in the world that's deprived because it hasn't got something feminine in it or about it. It's just a conviction I have that some kind of wholeness, of content, is a good thing and is possible. A religion that has a feminine component and a notion of the mother in the transcendental world is better than a religion that just has a father, a man, in it. I also—just in my nature and temperament, I suppose—believe in humility and in bowing down, and in 'we' rather than 'I'. I hate a *moi* situation, an egotism, a presumption, a *hubris*, and I'm using the bowing down to the mother as a way of saying that. About the only *enmity* I have is towards pride.

Is your avoidance of egotism anything to do with why, in perhaps a majority of your poems, you avoid contingent matters, family problems, social problems?

I don't think those problems important; I can't make it work. The poetry I love is some kind of image or visionary thing. What the hell do we know about the habits of life in any age from its poetry? Maybe from Chaucer, but then that's a special case. I don't know why I avoid . . . I've never had my children in any poems . . .

And yet many poets would wish to celebrate a family communion of some sort, or to find an identity in that context?

It's very difficult technically and artistically to do it. I mean, sure you can sit down and do it, but is it a poem? I had terrific interest in my youngsters when they were in the womb! There's one poem in *Door into the Dark* which isn't so good, called 'Mother', where a pregnant woman speaks; and the 'Act of Union' poem in *North* is a pregnancy poem. Those are, I suppose, the only kind of family poems I've written. It's part of the guilt of having fathered the pain as well as the child.

Much of your poetry speaks of atavism, genetic memories, about digging back into roots . . . I've always felt that this is very close to someone like Ted Roethke, who does it in 'The Lost Son' . . .

That's right.

Obviously he has a strong appeal for you.

Terrific.

And yet almost what's going on for Roethke is a Jungian idea of regression in order to reconstitute his own personality, to find himself because he can't face his being an adult, I suppose . . . Would it be unfair to apply such terms to you?

I don't know about that. I think part of Roethke's problem as a writer in those middle poems was that he was going into that kind of scientific language about the self. I said in a review I wrote that those 'Lost Son' poems weren't so much raids on the inarticulate as constructs for it; and what I meant was, there was a kind of *voulu* quality about the enterprise and I think that in such poems as 'Cuttings' and 'Growing', the whole thing's in those, and in the last poems, *The Far Field*. It's just a prejudice I have, but I think that Roethke—to use a phrase of Kavanagh's—views his soul from the outside in those poems; there's a kind of Freudian nod-and-wink to the reader, and it isn't a whole voice, it's the maker's voice, that is making up those poems.

I think that it's a very, very delicate matter for a writer—how to conceive and perceive himself, to what extent self-consciousness, self-knowledge, self-criticism, self-exposure, should be mixed or meshed; to what extent in an interview like this you should tell how much you know. You have to preserve a cellarful of life of your own.

In Roethke's case, there's surely a terrible sense of having to recover, to rehearse his own being at all.

I think that the drama and interest of the self may be the real subject, but in this country, the self is closely involved with the society that produces it, and it's bonded into a communal life. I don't know, I haven't entered into it too far. I've almost an anger at so much self being around; I find a lot of poetry by good poets about themselves boring as hell. You write books of poems because that is a fulfilment, a making; it's a making sense of your life and it gives achievement, but it also gives you a sense of growth.

What is important in a lot of your poems is this conjuring of a past time, a sort of communion with bases: is that exploit one which has intrinsic value, or do you see it as personally salutary or consolatory? In 'Gifts of Rain' you remark that it's 'for my children's sake'; do you regard your work as being—to use a Poundian phrase—of present use?

Unless it is, it's no good. Its first function is probably to appease yourself, to get it out. Now the appeasement quotient is probably the same in the worst, most sentimental writer and in a writer like Berryman or Eliot. They get up from the desk satisfied. But the second thing—and I think to discover this is part of your growth as a writer—is when you pass through the satisfactions of making into questions about what you make. And at that point you're endangered by self-consciousness, because you have to retain an innocence and a trust in the process if you're to keep going, a kind of spontaneity and impetus just in the doing of it. But I still think that you also have to question yourself about what is the efficacy of poetry.

There are two dialogues, one through the language with all the literate readers and with that pure delight in art itself, and that is perhaps the primary dialogue, and it's a pure pursuit of excellence—the covenant between you and the literate reader that excellence will be celebrated if it's arrived at. That is possibly fundamental. The second thing is, in what resides this excellence?—and then you're into: is it art or is it life? The pursuit of the verbal icon eventually leads you into a confrontation with the mess of the actual around you, and in this country we have had no shortage of actual mess. When I was in Glanmore I thought a lot about the function of writing. Dan Jacobson said to me once, 'You feel bloody well guilty about writing', and there is indeed some part of me that is entirely unimpressed by the activity, that doesn't dislike it, but it's the generations, I suppose, of rural ancestors—not illiterate, but not literary. They, in me, or I, through them, don't give a damn. I don't know whether that's a good thing or a bad thing.

Do you have any problem, then, of self-consciousness in writing?

That is never a problem, because I only write when I'm in the trance. It is a mystery of sorts. If you are possessed by a subject, if you have a subject in you . . . the thing moves.

When you do cast your poems upon the world, as it were, do you fear for them, fear that the critics will mismanage what you're saying?

No, I don't. For example, editors occasionally want help with choosing poems for an anthology, but I tend to leave it to them, even if they pick poems that I think are not my best. I do believe in the work finding—sinking, swimming—discovering its readers.

Do you regret any of your poems?

If I were doing a Selected Poems—which I'd prefer to a Collected Poems—there are poems that obviously aren't what you thought they were when you did them, and you'd want to scuttle them. I *was* to do a Selected Poems last year, and I hesitated and didn't do it for two reasons: one, that I think the publication of a Selected Poems isn't just a publishing convenience, it's a declaration of a certain stage of artistic command: in a sense, you crown yourself when you select and I didn't think I was ready to crown myself. The second thing was that I wasn't certain what shape I wanted to pop out of these first four books. I'm certain that up to *North*, that that was one book; in a way it grows together and goes together. There has been a good bit of commentary about the metaphor of digging and going back, but luckily that was unself-conscious . . . the kind of unself-consciousness that poets approaching the age of forty know they won't have again!

At what stage did you feel you'd completed a book? . . . just a certain accumulation of poems?

The first two books were like that, kind of eager to test the poems out, gather them up.

Were they culled from a much larger store of poetry?

A much larger store of verse, anyway. I think when I did *Wintering Out* I had certain vague notions of a theme, of language and so forth. Certainly I had a notion of *North*, the opening of *North*: those poems came piecemeal now and again, and then I began to see a shape. They were written and rewritten a lot. In a sense my writing habits changed, partly from having the time, partly being freelance in Wicklow, putting the notion of being a writer at the centre of the lived, day-to-day life, rather than being a teacher who came home to be a poet. It gave a terrific force to the activity. That was coming through some sort of barrier for me. I think that I consecrated myself at that point. There was a new conviction, a new dimension, and I thought of it as work and as a real life. I felt then the onset of some kind of confidence and trust. I want to say that I worked at the poems and treated them as important.

Is that to say that many of your poems before then had been occasional?

I'm trying to think . . . I began to push things a bit more deliberately after *Wintering Out*. But there are two kinds of activity and both I think are essential: one is a kind of speedy swoop, an excitement, and there's a certain type of poem that depends on that grace. The little place-name poems in *Wintering Out* came straight out. There are other little poems there, like 'Servant Boy' and 'Fodder', where the pleasure of the poem for me, and I think for anyone who gets anything out of them, is in the rustle of the language itself, the way it unfolds and plays, and that was also the actual feel of writing them, delight and pleasure. But then if you take a rhymed stanzaic poem, you're into a different kind of handling of the language. It's a different enterprise, when you begin to look for the truth, when you want to say your social truth rather than yield yourself to the suggestions and gifts of the poem. But to tell you the truth I have very few preconceived notions except that I know that one image will cross on another. Yet I don't know what way they'll cross, or what they'll bring forth.

Those poems you would consider lesser now, would you rather do over again in a kind of Audenesque way or would you cancel them?

I'd rather cancel than do them again . . . There's a poem in *Death of a Naturalist* which is a great favourite with teachers and gained some notoriety a couple of years ago (some M.P. scolded it for being on an exam paper), called 'The Early Purges', about drowning kittens . . . I think that poem is unresolved, and precisely because it's unresolved, it's a great poem for teachers because you don't have to deal with the poem, you can deal with the moral question raised in it. I think, if I were doing a Selected Poems, I would keep the first three or four stanzas of that, and dump the rest of it: the rest of it is a kind of commentary. So there are little things like that. But once the poems are in a book, they're there and I usually forget about them.

In the sense that many of your poems are concerned with anthropological questings, with rehearsals of a dead time, tombs and bodies, and so on, why do you take such a subject?

I think there's some kind of psychic energy that cries out for a home, and you have to build the house for it with the elements of your poetry, with the given elements of your imagery, and that imagery has to have a breath of life in it. The breath of life and those elements come together best with me when I'm dealing with certain kinds of things. A rebuke is delivered occasionally in a simple-minded way to these poems with rural or archaic images because they aren't engaging with the modern world . . . I think that's entirely a kind of teacherly notion. I'm not going to say that you shouldn't engage with the modern world, but the way an artist engages with the modern world is through the techniques of his art among other things; it doesn't have to be modern subject matter at all, I think.

The sensuous composition of the poem becomes its own validity?

Yes, I think so. It's much simpler if you think of something like painting: a painter can lift anything and make an image of it. For an up-market contemporary painter, sedge is as 'meaningful' as silicon chips.

If I say that your poetry often shows a sacramental view of the earth, would you think it a fair observation?

I think it would be. David Jones has nice notions of the 'sign', the artist is a sign-maker . . . I hesitate to talk about these things . . . I think what you're saying is right.

There must be a danger of sentimentalizing or even glamorizing a world . . .

Well, this is it . . .

. . . which in its own time must have been nasty, brutish, and short . . .

I'm not so sure whether it was any nastier. I think it was hard, maybe, but there was a kind of rhythm to it and a completeness to it. I'm not saying that it can come back or anything.

Some place you use the phrase, 'what had begun to feel like reverence', as if you were rebuking yourself for feeling too respectful . . .

That was in a poem about a severed head; I discovered the manuscript of that poem a while back, and it had ended at first with a kind of reverence, and the voice that came in when I revised was a rebuke to the literary quality of that reverent emotion, if you like. This is one of the paradoxes: you have to be wary of literary emotion, but the literary canons have to be respected! The voice has to break into real feeling rather than settling for a dying fall that has been there already in some other poem.

There must come a time—perhaps someone else has suggested it to you—that in attaining a nature mysticism, you're avoiding human truths and putting natural truths, whatever they may be, in their place?

There are no rules for writing poetry; each poet worth his salt goes on with his own thing. The tune isn't called for the poet, he calls the tune: it took me a long time to learn that too.

Were you ever worried by reviews, by specific criticisms?

My worry was slightly more complex. I was worried by getting a lot of praise and knowing you couldn't rely on it; while a lot of my contemporaries were getting no praise. I felt embarrassed. There was always a slave in my triumphal chariot, saying, 'You're mortal! You're mortal!' I was always at least as conscious of the slave behind me as I was of the tickertape, and I'm very grateful for that.

You said last night that Marie [Heaney's wife] is your first critic. Is she a severe one?

She's an exact critic; she's entirely instinctive and usually, therefore, exactly right. She has a tremendous nose for a falsity. I've fought with her about some poems, and I've changed a couple. They're usually crucial things . . . and occasionally she comes round to liking a poem. It's probably a matter of tone.

You published Stations *in a small uncommercial edition; why not to a wider public? Was that because of Marie's reservations about it?*

I did three or four of them in California, and in that year Geoffrey

Hill's *Mercian Hymns* arrived, and in some ways I hesitated. I began them in California because the nature mysticism stuff was hot on the ground and I was re-entering little spots of time, really. It was the pleasure of writing them up. Then, for a few weeks in June '74 a whole lot of memories came, and I wrote them down, and I went back to this short prose form. I got excited at the possibility of making a sequence out of them. I did them fast; apart from the three or four I had done already, I did them all within about five weeks. Then I hesitated because they seemed to stand half-way between being a coherent prose memoir and not being quite a sequence. And a number of people responded to them unflatteringly. Nevertheless at the time I was excited by them, and I thought the pamphlet publication was ideal. A lot of people say to me they should be verse.

Why didn't you make them verse?

I don't know why I didn't do them as verse. Marie doesn't like them because she thinks that they aren't realized or thrown free, that they are like private family memories, pious.

Towards the end you remark that 'I grew to love the manifold griefs of chanters and assuaging bows', which suggests that throughout the sequence you are recording how you were stung into poetry sometimes by fine memories, but sometimes too by fierce ones . . .

All I wanted there was a beautiful cadence; I wanted to summon the mournful memories of pipes. That rather rococo phrase came out of just the sound . . . attempting a verbal equivalent for that mournfulness of some Irish music.

The word 'assuaging' seems a favourite with you; can you say why?

It's the opposite of exacerbate. There is a kind of writing that sets out to exacerbate. But I believe that what peotry does to me is comforting . . . if I read the *Divine Comedy*, the *Purgatorio*, it's in the highest, widest, deepest sense, *comforting*, Great art is comforting, in some odd way. I think that art does appease, assuage.

Isn't there a place for art to affront the reader?

Yes, there is a function for that kind of work . . . and one might get round to it sooner or later. My temperament doesn't incline to anger very much.

Does your assurance about your work reflect a sense that you feel comfortable with your life?

The activity of writing originates very, very far down, and is affected by everything in your life, and it *should* affect everything in your life. I found in Glanmore, which I keep going back to as a period of confirmation, some kind of coming into home—I discovered there that you had to be really coherent, and you had to be in earnest, and significantly that was the first place I was able to write about the house I was living in. That was because Glanmore was *like* the original place. But talking about the comfort of life and home, I'm afraid of comfort, and at the same time I believe that man is made for it too. I would love to be able to write a poetry that had some kind of sureness and fullness and generosity, yet wasn't complacent in any way. I feel resources within myself of good nature that I've never got into my poetry. But maybe it's entirely mistaken to think that your muse can bring in everything.

I suppose many poets have worked from the dread and terror in their own lives . . .

Any amount of dread. Fear is the emotion that the muse thrives on. That's always there.

At what moment do you feel that your art has realized the personal emotion?

It all coheres in the act of writing. I think that the quality of your thinking and commitment and responsibility between the moments of writing is what will finally come through in the writing. One of Pound's 'A Few Don'ts' is 'Go in fear of abstractions', and I think that perhaps I took that too literally for a long time. I also have no gift for it, but whatever poetic success I've had has come from staying within the realm of my own imaginative country and my own voice, which is not an abstract thinking voice at all. So that has confirmed my belief in Pound's advice, but at the same time, for a kind of growth, you have to be prepared to extend your voice. That is what I had in mind at the end of the first section of *North* in 'Hercules and Antaeus', and to me Hercules represents another voice, another possibility; and actually behind that poem lay a conversation with Iain Crichton Smith, a very fine poet but essentially different from the kind of poet I am. He's got a kind of Presbyterian *light* about him. The image that came into my mind after the conversation was of me being a dark soil and him being a kind of bright-pronged fork that was digging it up and going through it. I got these notions of two kinds of intelligence . . . The Hercules-Antaeus thing came to seem like a myth of colonization almost—that Antaeus is a native, an earth-grubber, in touch with the ground, and you get this intelligent and superior interloper who debilitates the native by raising him, taking him out of his culture, his element, and leaving him without force. You could think about Ireland in those terms . . .

When it comes to writing, Hercules represents the possibility of the play of intelligence, that kind of satisfaction you get from Borges, the play and pattern, which is so different from the pleasures of Neruda, who's more of an Antaeus figure. That kind of thinking led into the poetry of the second half of *North*, which was an attempt at some kind of declarative voice. I think that you've arrived as a poet when you can use an intonation that could be called public. There's a difference between, say, 'The Wind Among the Reeds' and 'The Wild Swans at Coole', the voice of that latter personal lyric isn't a self-entranced voice. It's clear, bare . . . I use the word public because it's not inwardly turned, it's set *out*. I think that the first voice I have is an inward musing, entranced at its best, but I would love to master a voice that could *talk out* as well as go into a trance.

What about Frost?

I read a lot of Frost early on. There are two or three poems which for some reason keep close to me . . . from *North of Boston*, 'Home Burial' is extraordinary, its bareness and tremendous understanding.

Yes, the tension and struggle between the couple in that poem: the phrase, for example, 'Mounting until she cowered under him' . . .

Yes, and it has tremendous opening and closing words. At the same time, Frost too has that surrender, the entranced thing, in 'After Apple-Picking' which, even though it's an old chestnut, is delightful. He has two things: the capacity-to-surrender-to-the-gift poem, and he has the cunning (in the Elizabethan sense) to handle a poem and make it move in a public kind of way. I would love to write a poem like 'The Most of It', which may be in some ways—and this is a bit heretical—a better poem than 'The Second Coming'. It's the same shape, but Yeats cranks up the machinery and gives you the stage directions. There's nothing in Frost's poem as good as the opening of Yeats's poem, nothing as metrically powerful, and turbulent, but the middle of Yeats's poem, 'A vast image out of Spiritus Mundi troubles my sight' . . . Oh well, I take that back: we won't put them in competition: I withdraw those remarks! The Frost poem is a revelation. It's illiterate in many ways, but I think it's one of the high points, a poem housing power of some kind. It's not discourse, analysis, judgement, display; it moves by instinct, moves itself, moves the reader; a sense of connection and perhaps not much deliberation. Yet Frost always preserved a strong sense of the art itself; he always believed that poetry should be beautiful.

Getting back to your own work for a moment, I guess a constant in your work is a sense of loss, of childhood and so forth, which you can never recover, since you have been deracinated . . .

I wonder is it deracination? I'm very close to home. I've two homes: this house and the house where I was brought up. When I go back, my father and mother are still alive, my brothers and sisters still around the place, I merge into it. One deracinates oneself, and I'm not sure I have done so.

You've used the phrase 'inner emigré'.

Yes, I love that phrase. It's in 'Exposure', the last poem in *North*, where I had no security, no rails to run on except the ones I invented myself. That's an ideal situation; you're like a goalkeeper waiting for the world to fire balls at you, and you see things more urgently and clearly, and you think.

I think it was Jarrell who said about Stevens's poems that they were 'obsessed with lack' . . .

That's the writer before he's written the poem, isn't it! It's a feeling of hunger, lust . . .

You've said that the four volumes up to North *finish one phase for you: is that really wishful thinking?*

No, it's a matter of inclination and of age, and changes. I've some notions of the work I want to do, maybe longer, more orchestrated . . .

Can you enlarge on that?

No . . .

Can you tell me something about the forthcoming volume, Field Work*?*

There are two main groups in it: elegies and love poems. I think the centre of the book is the 'Glanmore Sonnets', which are about living in Glanmore, but also about choice and commitment, and they were able—perhaps for the first time—able to bring it some of the contingencies. They were very close to the actual concerns of day-to-day, and I think in them I learned something of how to speak in the first person out of the self, and the elegies are like that too. They are for friends. And then some of the love poems are the voice talking. 'Love poems' is a terrible phrase; 'poems about relationships' is a bit limp too perhaps . . . 'Marriage poems', call them. There's no reason why benign emotions shouldn't be able to find utterance.

Are you happy in the role of public bard, the performer?

Happy in it, but suspicious of it. This goes back to the *hubris*. I think you have to realize that you're at your best when the first person singular is a vehicle for other things. One thing I try to avoid ever saying at readings is '*my* poem'—because that sounds like a presumption. The poem *came, it came*. I didn't go and fetch it. To some extent you wait for it, you coax it in the door when it gets there. I prefer to think of myself as the host to the thing rather than a big-game hunter.

Is that why you won't tamper with a poem again once it's in print?

To some extent, yes. Also, I feel I'm disabled slightly once it's in print, I feel it's over, finished. But I hope that I never put a poem in a book that was dishonest; it may have been inept or flat or pointless.

What do you get from a public reading?

I tend to read the same poems nearly all the time, poems that touch, reach and hold an audience. Some poems I don't read because I don't think they have that reach to the back of the hall. 'Anahorish', for example, I never read—yet it's one of my favourites—because there's no place for an audience to get in. It doesn't address, it muses. It's a public ritual, a performance, and the poems should be suited for speaking. Like a sermon, a reading is a conventional mode of behaviour. There's often a triviality about readings and a lack of respect for poetry and for the audience: some poets do charming, entertaining poems, which sell everybody short.

You won't try out new work on an audience?

No, an audience will give you back only what you want to get. I don't understand what people mean when they talk of trying out new work. I don't believe that the reading process is part of the act of composition. Reading to schools I've found exhausting. For years I tried to make poetry seem ordinary (possibly because I began as a teacher in a non-literary environment) and then I took a reaction against that, because I found myself saying things about the poems that were very far from the core.

I suppose you're obliged to give simplistic paraphrases?

Well, it's no bother for me to give simple paraphrases because they're simple in the first place!

What about readings in America?

That taught me the dangers because in America you tend to do a lot of readings over a short period . . . nothing to do with exhaustion, but to do with sucking your own poems dry for yourself. They lose their mystery for you, and the lack of emotional charge continues into the next reading . . . it becomes without juice. I think poets don't read enough of other poets; I would dearly love to be asked to do that, read a selection of poems you like, Wyatt, Marvell, Yeats. In America there is a readiness and an eagerness for poetry and for writers. I have found good responses, a kind assent . . .

Do you draw much from Ted Hughes's work and comprehend it?

I think the kind of poems he writes don't disturb that central reverence. There's a tremendous dynamo . . . I think his energy comes out in the quality of the diction, powerful, violent diction, and there's a kind of anger at work. Hughes's voice, I think, is in rebellion against a certain kind of demeaned, mannerly voice. It's a voice that has no truck with irony because his dialect is not like that . . . I mean, the voice of a generation—the Larkin voice, the Movement voice, even the Eliot voice, the Auden voice—the manners of that speech, the original voices behind that poetic voice, are those of literate English middle-class culture, and I think Hughes's great cry and call and bawl is that English language and English poetry is longer and deeper and rougher than that. That's of a piece with his interest in Middle English, the dialect, his insisting upon foxes and bulls and violence. It's a form of calling out for more, that life is more. And of course he gets back from that middle-class school the enmity he implicitly offers. Ted may be accused of violence, of grotesquerie, but there is tenderness and reverence and seriousness at the centre of the thing. That comes out clearly in many of the poems . . . I mean, *Gaudete* is the most beautiful register of vegetation, almost every line has riches.

I'm a different kind of animal from Ted, but I will always be grateful for the release that reading his work gave me. I have gone through all that education about Eliot's bringing in irony and urban subject matter and intelligence, and nothing in that connected with the scripts written in my being. Then I read Hughes, Kavanagh, R. S. Thomas, and I realized their work was dealing with my world. One of the poets I got a charge out of early on was Hopkins, and Ted's poetry had that kind of linguistic energy, arrest and power, textures and surfaces. What I searched for in a poem like 'Death of a Naturalist' was that kind of texture and richness. I had a notion of poetry being like stained glass almost, although now I would like to be able to write a poetry that was like window glass. I find Ted personally powerfully creative, nurturing; I think he has understanding of people and creativity. I don't see him that often . . .

I suppose there's more camaraderie and give-and-take and sportiveness with others like Longley, Derek Mahon, Paul Muldoon. When I was in Belfast, we almost did committee work on each other's poems; they were circulated in manuscript and sat upon, and before you had a book out your poems had been graduated and the canon was settled. Indeed that extended as far as John Montague who lived in Paris, and then in Cork. I finally, I think, wanted to escape that, partly because I wanted to get to a situation where I was thinking for myself about my own poems. It's partly a matter of development, and development within the group too. Derek, who's a very pure poet, and Michael, had a much stronger sense of themselves as poets than I had when I met them. Their intonation and subject matter were more fixed and elegant, and there was a good deal of joking about my rural elements ... I remember Michael Longley wrote a parody called 'Heaney's Spade'!

What do you hope to get from this visit to America? ... to meet any younger poets?

I've no sense of the younger American poets at all ... I look forward to time; all I want is a few hours every day to sit and write, or not write.

GEOFFREY HILL

Can you tell me something about your background first?

I was born in a small market town in Worcestershire in 1932. I was an only child. My father was a police constable and remained so throughout his career; I believe that my father's father started work as a stoker on the Great Western Railway. He afterwards joined the police force and rose to be Deputy Chief Constable of Worcestershire, which was the highest position one could then rise to from the ranks. He was an impressive man. I felt considerably in awe of him, without feeling particularly close. On my mother's side I'm descended from artisans in the traditional cottage-industry of nail-making. As a child and young woman my grandmother was a nailer, making hand-made nails. I felt very close to her; I realize retrospectively how close the attachment was. During my childhood my mother was seriously ill on two occasions, and I lived with my grandmother at those times, in her tiny cottage at the end of a row. It had a small garden with an ancient damson tree and an old shed which still contained my dead grandfather's carpenter's tools. My mother's family was Baptist, and when I was born my mother still belonged to the Baptist Church, but when I was three my father became police constable in a village about three miles north of the town in which I was born and my mother joined the Church of England there. I sang in the church choir from about the age of seven until I went up to Oxford.

Do you feel your parents and grandmother had a great influence on you? Was your adolescence, for example, a period of reaction against them and their assumptions about the life you might pursue?

My father and mother both left school at the age of thirteen, but although there was no academic tradition on either side of the family there was a deep care and concern for education as a way of 'bettering' oneself. My parents were not in any way 'serious' readers, but they encouraged my own reading.

So there was no question of going against the grain when you went on to Oxford?

No, I swam with the stream of their expectations, and of course with the expectations of the whole British educational system, in which a child who shows any lively aptitude for a certain subject is then schooled into the future professional exploitation of that aptitude. If it's only an aptitude, perhaps that doesn't matter too much; but gifts tend to be seduced the same way. It's a system about which many of us might now have reservations, but these are the reservations of hindsight; it was very difficult for any child or his parents situated as we were, in the late forties and early fifties, to have that kind of prescient understanding which might have guided one into a different course.

Did you like the experience of Oxford, or were you a loner discovering works of literature for yourself?

I felt socially very much isolated and ill-at-ease for the first two years, but in my third year the publication of my Fantasy Press pamphlet in the autumn of 1952 brought me to the notice of the Oxford poets of the day. I remained ill-at-ease socially, but made and kept several good friends. My experience was not the unalloyed enjoyment which it seems to have been for quite a number of my contemporaries. There were some occasions of happiness, but I would think on balance that the unhappiness outweighed the happiness.

Did you discuss your work with contemporaries?

We never formed anything like a group or a movement. Our discussions were entirely informal, and more often than not convivial. As for the intellectual stimulus, I worked very hard at the orthodox English Language and Literature syllabus of that time. There was of course very little opportunity for encountering contemporary literature on that syllabus, but I had in any case made my own discoveries long before I went up to Oxford.

On a shopping-trip to Birmingham, when I was about fifteen, my father bought me Oscar Williams's *Little Treasury of Modern Verse* together with the *Collected Poems* of A. E. Housman, and I carried the Williams anthology in my jacket pocket all over Worcestershire for several years until it disintegrated: I think there was probably a time when I knew every poem in that anthology by heart. My devotion to modern poetry thus began long before I went up to Oxford and it's at least to the credit of Oxford that it didn't kill it.

There was no particular tutor who nourished your interest in poetry or galvanized your work?

My tutors were invariably kind and helpful within the limits of the syllabus, but I think I can honestly say that any exploration of modern poetry or any furthering of my own creative work was made quite independently of them. I think this is quite as it should be. I don't think it should be the function of an academic tutor either to excite the young poet's creativity or interfere with the course it takes. It would surely be a rather low-key involvement which would need to be excited by outside advice of that kind. There's certainly no kind of reproach whatsoever in my tone when I say that I took my creative course quite independently of any tutorial advice. One obviously owes a debt which is very difficult to define to one's immediate contemporaries: conversation, exchange of views, mutual informal criticism. It would again be fair to say that I knew then that I was unlike my contemporaries in what I was doing, and they in turn realized that what I was doing was very different from what they were doing.

Can you say how your interests diverged: was it your subject matter or a predilection for certain areas of thought?

The poetry written by most of the 'promising' poets of the fifties seemed to me to stem from a basic misconception about the nature of poetry and language, and I must say that my views have changed very little since then. It seemed to me that young poets of that time were writing poetry of one or two kinds, neither of which was my kind. They were either Empsonian in the most arid sense, writing cerebral conundrums, a travesty of

Empson's real gifts; or they were narrating amorous adventures and travel anecdotes in language that was the equivalent of painting-by-numbers. I sensed intuitively that I really cared for neither of those alternatives. My basic intuitive sense has remained remarkably consistent in the succeeding thirty years.

Did you look to certain kinds of literature, such as nineteenth-century non-fiction, to inform your work?

No, that was a much later discovery. I was of course excited by the Metaphysical poets. Given the pre-eminence of the Metaphysicals in the education of a sixth-form boy of the period, it was only to be expected. Of the Metaphysicals, I believed I most admired Donne, but I was probably more haunted by Vaughan and Herbert. My unorthodox discovery was Isaac Rosenberg, whose work I first encountered in a review in Peter Russell's periodical, *Nine*. I immediately bought the *Selected Poems* published by Chatto, which I read avidly. The poem which particularly moved me began 'A worm fed on the heart of Corinth,/Babylon and Rome...' That particular poem gripped me in a deep and abiding way. I also discovered and became tremendously excited by the poetry of Christopher Smart. In its first printing my poem 'Genesis' was sub-titled 'A Ballad of Christopher Smart'. I knew the work of William Blake and of Housman, who was a fellow townsman of mine. Before I knew anything at all about the psychology of Housman, I knew what his 'Shropshire' meant to him at an intuitive level again—because the Shropshire hills were the western horizon of the village landscape of my childhood. If you stood at the top of the field opposite our house you looked right across the Severn Valley to the Clee Hills and the Welsh hills very faint and far off behind them, and this was the landscape of Housman's own childhood. He had in fact been born in a house which (I think I'm right in recalling) was the last house on my father's beat.

During the formative years of my childhood travel was very considerably restricted because of the war. We could not in any case have afforded a car on my father's pay, but even bus, coach and train journeys were something of a rarity in those days. Although Shropshire and Herefordshire are so close to my birthplace that not to have visited them seems ridiculous, the fact is that, summer after summer, I gazed into those strange, far-off lands as the child Housman had done. I think it's entirely due to the fact that Housman was hardly ever in Shropshire that the atmosphere of his literary 'Shropshire' is so curiously clear yet remote.

I'd like to ask you further about your love for Vaughan and Herbert . . . and Crashaw?

Not Crashaw at that time; I shared the common prejudice against Crashaw. It's only in very recent years that I've come to an understanding and admiration of his work.

Did your feeling for the Metaphysicals run to sharing their intellectual passions, or was your concern on a technical level?

There was an intellectual strength in the Metaphysicals which obviously appealed to me, but that was only part of the appeal, since their intellectual strength is always complemented by a quality which is best summed up in Milton's phrase about poetry being more simple, sensuous and passionate than either logic or rhetoric. It was their fusion of intellectual strength with simple, sensuous and passionate immediacy which drew me to them, and that is an immediacy quite different from narrative or anecdotal immediacy, totally different from that spontaneous overflow of powerful feelings which—taken out of context—is one of the statements that has most seriously misled post-Romantic 'poetry lovers'. Out of context, Wordsworth's phrase has a totally different meaning from its meaning in context: I'm not blaming Wordsworth for any abuse to which his terms have been put.

Did you start your teaching career at Leeds?

Yes. I have taught elsewhere on secondment—in the USA and West Africa—and in recent years have lectured and read my work fairly widely, in the USSR, India, Canada, Europe.

Have you found that teaching militates at all against your creative work?

I can point to one or two instances where my professional work has had a beneficial effect on my creative work, in the sense of putting in my way happy discoveries which I might not have made if I'd not been a teacher of English Literature. It was a happy accident that in order to give a lecture course on Shakespeare I found myself re-reading the *Henry VI* plays at exactly the right time; discovering the power of a certain kind of rhetoric which I'd been educated to think of as inferior to Shakespeare's later work. This came at a time when my thoughts were beginning to stir towards the writing of the sequence 'Funeral Music'.

But in general you've not found that your students' expectations have led you to qualify or modify your creative work?

I've not found that anybody's expectations have led me to qualify or modify my own work. Writing about the poetry of Jacoponi da Todi, Evelyn Underhill says that 'of Jacoponi as a poet we may say generally that in him poetry turns towards the people but does not capitulate to them', and this seems to me to sum up perfectly the relationship that ought to exist between any creative writer and what is dangerously and equivocally termed the reading public. Poetry should, ideally, turn towards the people, but, the world being what it is, there's an ignorant expectation that one must succumb to a lowest common denominator of demand. My own feeling is that a considerable danger for the poet lies at either extreme. If he pretends to be wholly unaware of any other mind or spirit with whom he would communicate, then he's in peril of lapsing into a dangerous solipsism. At the other extreme, if he trims his work in any way to some real or supposed expectation, then it seems to me that the danger is just as great.

You would second Coleridge's enunciation that the reader should be a fellow labourer, but are you also working towards a notion of an ideal reader?

In a sense. I'm not so arrogant as to suppose or to suggest that I'm indifferent to criticism, but on the other hand I'm not so humble as to say that I read criticism in order to learn about my mistakes and benefit from them. But I have the recollection of occasionally having read a piece which does seem uncannily in harmony with one's own intention ... if one can speak of an intention, which makes the process sound more direct and mechanical than it really is.

Do you feel, though, that any particular poems were predetermined or preconceived, or is it the case that your insights and concerns always realize themselves solely in the process of composition, in the application of intelligence and technique?

It's a mixture of the two. I've gone sometimes for ten years knowing—in a curiously precise way—that something is waiting to be written; the only obstacle is a total inability to write it. It would be too fanciful to call it a Platonic shape, but I can't think of any other way of describing that strange mixture of nagging and calming allurement—sometimes clear, sometimes hazy, but definitely unattainable for the time being. Then, if I'm lucky, various germinal phrases or a hint of rhythm or something as minutely technical as the cadence of an enjambment will begin to stir, and for a time I have to be content to let the work grow by this process of accretion. Again, if I'm lucky, there will come a point when things begin to click into shape, and I can push ahead at a somewhat faster rate, but never very fast. I now have a long run of notebooks and, consulting them, I can see how long it has taken in many instances for first ideas to finalize themselves. Such phrases and rhythms and cadences are ganglions in which intellect and emotion and the minute necessary technical adjustments are held together in some way that one knows is full of possibility. But, as I say, for weeks, months, and in some cases years, one cannot discover what that potential is.

Can it be summed up as a kind of brooding?

Brooding is a useful word because of its range of connotation: it can suggest both an outward-turned creativity and an inward-turned depression. One can brood positively, in order to foster and bring forth, or one can brood in order to shut out and negate, and in choosing the word 'brood' to try to define the emotions and the problems of writing you are of course using the word in a richly poetic sense.

In the process of seminal meditation, do you find that you know the subject from the start, or does it emerge from the passion and the brooding?

I know the subject but I don't know the argument. I don't think I've ever conceived a poetic argument as a thing in itself which merely required words to embody it. I can only discover my argument in discovering the words for it. There's a phrase of William Blake's from *Jerusalem*, 'the struggles of entanglement with incoherent roots', and in moments of either elation or depression I feel that the phrase could stand as an epigraph to my whole writing life. One can take 'incoherent roots' either literally or figuratively, and I suppose the particular excitement of *Mercian Hymns* was to find that I was meditating on my roots in a double sense.

So you'd refute the accusation of some critics that you've elected certain prefigured intellectual formulations which you then chiselled into words?

I would not only have to refute that kind of unfavourable criticism, I'd also be obliged to qualify strongly even some kinds of favourable comment which credit me with a higher degree of ratiocinative power than I think I possess. I am immodest enough to think that I have certain skills, but I don't number among them either the mastery of dialectic or the forensic arts.

Have any specific poems come to you in terms of gifts, as it were?

I think there comes a point of breakthrough in every work which is not unrelated to exhaustion. A certain kind of exhaustion can be a great gift to a creative artist, but it's not the exhaustion which comes from the attrition of daily life, for that is nothing but destructive. It's the kind of exhaustion that is involved with prolonged and intensive labour on the work in hand. Exhaustion is rather like Time in Shakespeare's last plays; it can release the creative faculty from the constraining grip of all sorts of superficial inhibitions: it can release quite unexpected graces of inspiration.

I do believe most profoundly in inspiration, but it has nothing to do with the vulgar notion of inspiration which supposes that Chopin sat at his piano listening to rain pattering on the roof and was immediately inspired to write the so-called 'Raindrop' Prelude. I believe that there must be such a thing as inspiration because I've experienced it. This inspiration comes at the end of a work, when maybe only a word or a phrase or a few sentences are wanting, and they will not come, and you struggle for hours, days, even weeks, in agony of mind trying a hundred variants, and suddenly the word or phrase is there with that marvellous click like a closing box that Yeats talks about.

Is the exhaustion you speak of akin to entrancement?

There's a significant difference. I've only once ever written in a way to delight the sentimental biographer, and that was in the last stages of preparing my version of Ibsen's *Brand.* The last lines I wrote were the last lines of Act III: the decision of Brand to sacrifice the life of his child, to remain in the icy valley, and Agnes's bitter acquiescence with that decision. Of course the kind of labour I put into *Brand* was for me a unique departure, since I was working to schedules and deadlines in a way I had never done in my own poetry. I was driving myself night after night into the early hours of the morning after a full day's teaching and administration. Labour and excitement combined to induce a state of euphoria, what you would call 'entrancement', a kind of quite falsely mystical ecstasy, which was most interesting to observe in oneself. At the same time, I knew exactly why I was in that state, and I observed myself with interest and not without humour. That's the only time I've ever found myself in that state, and I do not in any way overrate it.

With my own poetry, when I'm able to write it, the process seems a slow, common craftsmanship, an ordinary occurrence. There comes a moment, after all the anxiety and doubt, when one is working to a conclusion and feels fully in command of the material and the situation. Obstacles will occur, but you do not at a deep level lose confidence. But in those terrible troughs—which in retrospect are called 'lying fallow', but while they occur one must call sterility—one looks back with bewilderment at those periods when one seemed able to exercise a perfectly ordinary craftsmanship; and these periods then take on almost a miraculous dimension. In writing, one is surprised by joy when what one thought one was going to write and what one has actually written come together in the closest possible way.

But those things must also diverge at times?

The joyous surprise is to arrive at a point one 'had in mind' but to find that one has said it so much better than one could possibly have hoped. One lives for so long with an approximate blurred shape, and yet finally finds that the whole thing has come into very sharp focus by the gift of a word or phrase.

But do you find that the poem fully and finally realizes itself, and that you rarely have to alter things, perhaps after publication?

I don't think I would release a poem unless I felt at the time totally satisfied with it. Of course, like others, I've had the bitter experience of discovering, much later, that the work contained previously unsuspected howlers. The only good reason for a poet to interfere with his poem once it's in print is a penitential reason of that kind. Earlier work should not be changed to accommodate changed theological, philosophical or political views. Whether through jolted *amour propre* or for some more exemplary reason, one is wounded by the discovery of technical vulnerabilities in one's work, and should perhaps be allowed to erase them. A solecism can perhaps be removed, a precise or more resonant word can be substituted for an imprecise or dud word. I do dislike it very much when a poet interferes with a poem which I've loved for years. John Crowe Ransom was notorious for altering his own poems; and, as I recall, there were a couple of versions of Allen Tate's 'Ode to the Confederate Dead' in circulation at one time. I think he was justified, since he was altering the poem only for technical reasons and the final version is the best. I can't say the same of Ransom's 'Prelude to an Evening' or some of Auden's revisions.

In one of your own 'Lachrimae' sequence, you changed the word 'outwit' to 'revoke'.

The phrase is 'None can revoke your cry', and I would have thought there's a much greater play between 'revoke' and 'cry'. That's a technical second thought which came to me between the poem's first appearance in *Agenda* and its publication in book form. I'd have been happier if it had been a first thought.

Since you have resolutely disavowed egotism and self-expression as bases for writing poetry, can you characterize your work in terms of your own remark—which I perhaps rather unfairly take out of context—that 'the nature of a man's occupation, the range of his expectations and the limits of his security might well be influential in forming the rhythms and cadences of his speech'?

In the context from which you take those remarks I'm trying to define certain limitations; I try to explain why the rhetoric of a man I otherwise very much admire, the Tory radical Richard

Oastler, is in one or two instances as bad as it is. I was criticizing Oastler's rhetoric on rather different grounds from those advanced by Cecil Driver in his admirable biography. He agrees that certain aspects of that rhetoric are dangerously demagogic, but he tries to attribute it to disposition and personality, and I think I fairly say that those are insecure terms on which to build speculation. I would have thought that one could not profitably approach the nature of a poet's speech in quite those terms, because the nature of true poetic speech is the attempt to transfigure some of the negative liabilities of speech into more positive form. My admiration for Oastler and the whole radical Tory tradition that he represents is considerable: I find it one of the most attractive political traditions of the nineteenth century, and something quite apart from what we now know as Conservatism. Modern Conservatism, which is Whiggery rampant, could be beneficially instructed by radical Toryism, but of course won't let itself be. Conservatives conserve nothing.

But—if I can reframe the question—do you disavow that poetry has anything to do with the personality of the writer?

No, I don't. I deny that it has anything to do with the display of the personality of the writer. The problem we're up against is the debauching of the word 'personality' in modern parlance, the sense in which the term is used in canting commodity speech—such as 'TV personality'—the turning of mannerisms into a saleable commodity. Of course the true poet must repudiate such debasement. But if, by personality, we mean the true selfhood of a person, then it would be foolishness to deny the connection between poetry and a man or woman's self. I still see no reason to quarrel with the celebrated passage from Eliot's 'Tradition and the Individual Talent', which does not deny personality but enters caveats against the false equation of poetry with a certain kind of luxuriating in personality: 'Poetry is not a turning loose of emotion, but an escape from emotion; it is not the expression of personality, but an escape from personality. But, of course, only those who have personality and emotions know what it means to want to escape from these things.'[1] The

[1] F. Kermode (ed.), *Selected Prose of T. S. Eliot*, Faber, 1975, p. 43.

word 'escape' was not a particularly happy choice and left Eliot vulnerable to misinterpretation, but if we can accept that he means 'transcendence' I see very little to quarrel with in the statement.

The transcendence of personality in art presupposes an intensity and richness of personality in the creator. But any discussion of this question is bedevilled by a problem poets are constantly encountering: the debasement of language. Poetry is not self-expressiveness of a vulgarly spontaneous kind. The crux of the matter turns upon creative expression of personality versus commodity exploitation of personality. There's a fine ironic phrase of Nietzsche's about 'this delight in giving a form to oneself as a piece of difficult, refractory and suffering material'. In such a phrase the difficulties, refractoriness and suffering of the personality and the difficult and refractory nature of language itself are seen to cohere.

Do you feel there is truth in C. H. Sisson's remark, 'There is in Hill a touch of the fastidiousness of Crashaw, which is that of a mind in search of artifices to protect itself against its own passions,'[1]—or would you refute or qualify it?

Leaving aside its applicability to myself or otherwise, it is an acute comment on a certain kind of poetry which, I would agree, is perhaps supremely represented in the work of Crashaw. But 'a mind in search of artifices to protect itself' might imply something perhaps a little too deliberately predetermined, too hygienic. I would find it hard to disagree with the proposal that form is not only a technical containment, but is possibly also an emotional and ethical containment. In the act of refining technique one is not only refining emotion, one is also constantly defining and redefining one's ethical and moral sensibility. One is constantly confronting and assessing the various kinds of moral and immoral pressures of the world, but all these things happen simultaneously in the act of self-critical decision.

Do you have strong feelings about the function of art and poetry, or do you feel that when we look to art for consolation, sublimation or transcendence we should remain sceptical about its value?

[1] 'Geoffrey Hill', *Agenda*, vol. 13 no. 3, Autumn 1975, p. 27.

What is wrong with accepting both parts of that proposition? To succeed totally in finding consolation in art would be to enter a prelapsarian kingdom. Father Christopher Devlin has a very fine phrase to define the themes of Hopkins's sermons—'the lost kingdom of innocence and original justice', which is a lovely resonant phrase; and without in any way aligning myself hubristically with Hopkins, I would want to avail myself of Devlin's phrase, because I think there's a real sense in which every fine and moving poem bears witness to this lost kingdom of innocence and original justice. In handling the English language the poet makes an act of recognition that etymology is history. The history of the creation and the debasement of words is a paradigm of the loss of the kingdom of innocence and original justice.

If we can accept that image to any degree, then it seems to me that we can simultaneously accept the genuine possibility of consolation in art and be sceptical about the possibility of ultimate consolation. After all, scepticism is a totally different thing from cynicism. A society which provides such solid rewards for the vacuousness of the television personality is so centrally and orthodoxly cynical that scepticism belongs with poetry as a kind of marginal resistance to it. Therefore the oxymoronic nature of our world produces a resistant paradox, which is that the poem, which in itself may not contain a grain of scepticism, may nonetheless belong with certain kinds of constructive scepticism as one of the instruments of resistance to the drift of the age.

Do you actually hold certain religious, philosophical or ethical convictions which you think it is not the place of poetry to formulate as absolute statements?

If poetry has any value, that value must presuppose the absolute freedom of poetry to encompass the maximum range of belief or unbelief. I would have thought that this problem had been solved already for European poets by the poetry of the Psalms, the Book of Job, and the *Divine Comedy*.

One critic has said that your poetry has the air of mystical utterance but lacks a true feeling for the passion of religion. Could you comment on that criticism?

Isn't such a comment based on a radical misunderstanding of

the relation of poet to topic, on the most naïve and simplistic sense of how poetry functions, on the supposition that the poem is merely a vessel to contain the spontaneous efflux of some kind of direct, unqualified, unmodified, unfiltered personal spasm? The complex nature of religious experience, and religious sectarianism of a great number of different kinds, is an essential part of the complex history of Europe. Its effects have been felt both in the broadest and the most minute senses; the fate of nations and the happiness or wretchedness of individuals. I really do not see that it indicates any shortcoming in a poet to be moved by the phenomena of religious experience both in its historical perspective and in more immediate examples. Since a failure to truly grasp experience and substance is one of the characteristic failings of human nature, I would have thought that the lyric poet with any psychological and dramatic sense is quite properly involved with that kind of distancing and failure.

The criticism does imply that one should take up an attitude of commitment.

The short answer to that is that the criticism is coarse and obtuse. If critics accuse me of evasiveness or the vice of nostalgia, or say that *I* seem incapable of grasping true religious experience, I would answer that the grasp of true religious experience is a privilege reserved for very few, and that one is trying to make lyrical poetry out of a much more common situation—the sense of *not* being able to grasp true religious experience. I'm accused of being nostalgic when I'm in fact trying to draw the graph of nostalgia. The painter Francis Bacon said somewhere that he was 'trying to paint the track left by human beings like the slime left by a snail', and it seems to me that in poetry also one is trying to trace the track left by human beings, which is full of false directions and self-pity and nostalgia as well as lust, wrath, greed and pride.

Could you possibly enlarge a little on why you're drawn so strongly to the subjects of mysticism and martyrology: is it that the possibilities of faith and doubt form a crux of the human condition?

I am interested in mysticism as an exemplary discipline, and I'm also interested in the psychopathology of the false mystical experience. Of course no one has been more accurate in defining and warning against the perils of false mysticism than the medieval mystics; the genuine mystic is usually a tough, practical, level-headed man, and I think those iron-disciplined mystics—unless their charity overcame their scorn—would have hard things to say of the more self-indulgent mystical cults of the present day.

Would you feel that your poetry is necessarily an art of equivocation, since your subjects are not available to synthesis?

Equivocation was a form of casuistry adopted by men under duress to try to avoid what the Elizabethans called the 'bloody question' and its inevitable consequences of torture and death. I sympathize with anyone who would equivocate in that situation; but in other circumstances I think there would be less excuse. Perhaps I'm failing to see the slant of your question.

I suppose what I'm implying is that critics are often looking for resolute answers and assertions where it is a necessary condition of your subject matter to be irresolute.

Yes, but that's still not equivocation. I resent the implication—taking the dictionary definition of equivocation—of my using words in a double sense in order to mislead.

But would you resent the criticism that you address yourself to subjects in an ambiguous way?

Yes, I would, though perhaps not as vehemently. I query the idea that I 'address myself to subjects', which seems to imply some kind of settled policy. It may be that the subjects present themselves to me as being full of ambiguous implications, but this is surely a different matter. The ambiguities and scruples seem to reside in the object that is meditated upon.

Martyrdom is an act of witness; not every person who is killed unjustly is necessarily witnessing, though I suppose the liturgy of the Church, in choosing to regard the Holy Innocents as martyrs, has rebuked my point in anticipation. But to take the group who have most interested me in recent years, the Catholic martyrs of the age of Elizabeth I, there seems there to have been what I might call a pedagogy of martyrdom, a scholastic process of training towards that deliberate goal. I do find the psychology of that kind of procedure fascinating, and of course chilling in many ways.

It comes down to a schooling in self-destruction, doesn't it, supposedly for the best of all possible reasons?

Yes, and it does indicate an ability to overcome the animal self, which I think has been marvellously caught in Eliot's line about the 'reluctance of the body to become a *thing*'. It's simultaneously illuminating and perplexing. The overcoming of the animal fear of death seems to me an achievement which may be inspiring in some ways but is profoundly chilling in others. I really can't see why one's brooding on that very ambiguity should be called equivocation; I do not see why the making of lyric poetry out of one's mixed feelings of attraction and repulsion should be dismissed in some obtuse way as a failure to grasp true and passionate religious experience.

Can you characterize the appeal you found in the poetry of sixteenth-century Counter-Reformation Spain, and how it informed your poetry?

I can only answer that by taking you through a process. We've not yet talked about my deep and passionate love of music, and my envy of the composer, who seems to have several advantages over the poet: he unites solitary meditation with direct, sensuous communication to a degree greater than the poet. In the first instance musical composition is the scratching of pen upon paper but then those signs are translated into the immediate, sensuous configurations of sound, the actual iconic presence of brazen instrument and shaken air, in a way that poetry can only envy. I discovered at a relatively late date that my feelings about that were Schopenhauerian and Nietzschean, but it endorses my constant argument that I do see poetry as a sensuous art.

My sequence called 'The Pentecost Castle' originated about ten years ago when I heard a harpsichord recital by Rafael Puyana, which included a piece by the sixteenth-century Spanish composer Antonio de Cabezón, 'Diferencias sobre el canto del Caballero'. It struck me as a piece of such stunning power and beauty that from then on I was entirely enthralled by it, and I struggled until I could make some competent show of it on the piano. I then discovered that the theme for these magnificent variations was a little folk tune which gave Lope de Vega the motif for his play *El Caballero de Olmedo*. Again, by a lucky accident, I had been browsing through the *Penguin Book of Spanish Verse* and had discovered one of the religious sonnets of Lope de Vega which enchanted me so much that I began to try to translate it. These two figures, Cabezón and Lope de Vega, were united by this tiny thread of folk song. I began to read my way into Lope de Vega's work—that play in particular—and I pursued every clue I could between the Cabezón piece and that snatch of folk song. The words of the little folk song became the first lyric of the 'Pentecost Castle' sequence.

As I read around the play and the poetry of that period I found one or two other folk songs which I also felt moved to adapt, and I felt sufficiently stirred and delighted to want to try my hand at writing lyrics in the manner of the period. The Lope de Vega sonnet became the final poem of another sequence, 'Lachrimae', and the impulse to write that sequence arose as much out of a passionate love for the music of John Dowland as out of my interest and admiration for the life and writings of St. Robert Southwell. Having said what I can about the first impulse and the raw process of working towards the composition of both sequences, I should also say that the essential meaning of each sequence is contained in the very carefully chosen epigraphs to each of them.

The little drama of 'The Pentecost Castle' is fairly subliminal: could you say at what point it became apparent to you?

I wrote the first two lyrics, and then the rest followed over about eighteen months, not necessarily in the final order. It's a hinted drama. One or two critics have suggested that a coherent, consecutive drama is being conveyed: I don't think it's so. I had no such intention; there's no plot but there are little shadowy hints of one. The kind of poetry I was first of all freely translating and then imitating turns within such a narrow compass of conventional phraseology and idiom that clues seem to be offered which are not necessarily clues to some perfectly articulated drama.

Did you immediately see the Lope de Vega sonnet which now stands last in 'Lachrimae' as forming part of that sequence?

No, the idea occurred to me some time later. There was quite a gap in time, but then I wrote the other six sonnets relatively quickly by my standards, in about twelve months. The 'Christian Architecture' sequence was much more sporadic in the writing; I began it some time before 1973, and I wanted it to be a more extended sequence from the beginning. That sequence took about six years to complete.

I see the 'Christian Architecture' sequence as—to borrow your phrase from the notes to 'Funeral Music'—both a commination and alleluia again. Would that be right in your view?

Yes. I think the sad serenity and elegance of the eighteenth-century country house landscape was bought at a price: not only the sufferings of English labourers but also of Indian peasants. Again, critics who think I've succumbed to nostalgia for that landscape cannot have looked with sufficient closeness to the texture of the sequence. The celebration of the inherited beauties of the English landscape is bound, in the texture of the sequence, with an equal sense of the oppression of tenantry. If one writes lyrics of which nostalgia is an essential element, naïve or malicious critics will say that the nostalgia must be one's own. There are, however, good political and sociological reasons for the floating of nostalgia: there's been an elegiac tinge to the air of this country ever since the end of the Great War. To be accused of exhibiting a symptom when, to the best of my ability, I'm offering a diagnosis appears to be one of the numerous injustices which one must suffer with as much equanimity as possible.

To celebrate a thing is not necessarily to endorse it, or to connive with the social system which produced it?

Some people seem incapable of making this very elementary distinction.

Can you describe how and why you came to write Mercian Hymns, *and why you chose to write the sequence in the form of prose poems?*

They're versets of rhythmical prose. The rhythm and cadence are far more of a pitched and tuned chant than I think one normally associates with the prose poem. I designed the appearance on the page in the form of versets. The reason they take the form they do is because at a very early stage the words and phrases began to group themselves in this way. I did immediately see it as an extended sequence, and it did come quite quickly for me—in three years, which is rapid by my standards. My second book, *King Log*, was nine years in the making.

I'd like to quote the panegyric Harold Bloom wrote by way of introducing the American edition of your work, Somewhere Is Such A Kingdom*:* 'Mercian Hymns*, despite the limpidity of its individual sections, is the subtlest and most oblique of his works. It is not only hard to hold together, but there is some question as to what it is "about", though the necessary answer is akin to* The Prelude *again: Hill has at last no subject but his own complex subjectivity, and so the poem is "about" himself, which turns out to be an exchange of gifts with the "Muse of History".' Are those the terms in which you see the work?*

I think it is less solipsistic than that description suggests. I was not merely interested in the phenomenon of my own sensibility, I was genuinely interested in the phenomenon of King Offa and of the rise and fall of the Kingdom of Mercia. My feeling for Offa and Mercia can scarcely be disentangled from my mixed feelings for my own home country of Worcestershire. Since Offa seems to have been on the whole a rather hateful man who nonetheless created forms of government and coinage which compel one's admiration, this image of a tyrannical creator of order and beauty is, if you like, an objective correlative for the inevitable feelings of love and hate which any man or woman must feel for the *patria*. The murderous brutality of Offa as a political animal seems again an objective correlative for the ambiguities of English history in general, as a means of trying to encompass and accommodate the early humiliations and fears of one's own childhood and also one's discovery of the tyrannical streak in oneself as a child. Here again one is speaking of those characteristics which one holds in common with one's fellow beings.

There is a sense in which you saw your own experience as being personated in Offa . . . you saw a correspondence on one level?

Yes, but I would have thought in a very unremarkable way. One is quite willing to point out that of course elements of one's own childhood experience, one's delights and humiliations, the discovery of the good and the bad in oneself, merged with the delighted discovery of the existence of Offa and this strange kingdom almost lost to history, but quite understandably one is resisting all the time any assumption that this has anything to do with the 'confessional' mode. This is one of the hazards of interrogation and discussion, one is surrounded by clouds of false witness: one is not only trying to describe as accurately as possible what one felt and how one worked, but one is simultaneously having to try to purge the very language of both long-established and recent perversions of its meaning and implications.

Yes, there are so many degrees and dimensions of speaking of oneself. Could you comment on how you came to write 'The Songbook of Sebastian Arrurruz', and your intentions in writing it, including perhaps its sense of humour?

It's good of you to mention the humour, since I think there's been the constant presence of humour throughout my poetry, and even a light-heartedness which I think many critics have either wilfully neglected to notice or innocently overlooked. There's nothing unique or original in creating the idea of an imaginary poet or writer and in giving him a small body of work. My main inspiration for the idea was in the work of Antonio Machado, who had created an 'apocryphal professor' called Juan de Mareina and an imaginary poet-philosopher called Abel Martín. I gave Arrurruz the chronology 1868–1922, which enabled him to celebrate the centenary of his birth on the date of publication of my second book, which was advantageous to both of us (we shared a celebration party), and also enabled him to die on the very threshold of modernity, without having had the advantage of reading *The Waste Land* or *Ulysses*. Arrurruz is a shy sensualist with a humour that could be said to balance the sensuality except that the finer nuances have been lost in translation.

Was it simply an excursion of fantasy for you, or did you feel implicated in his experience?

No more implicated in his experience possibly than any author would feel implicated in the loves and sufferings of his characters. I would have thought it's an area of common implication. A sequence of love poems, whether given to a fictional character or not, is surely the area where everybody can say that Keats's axioms have been proved upon the pulses.

Could you explain how you came to terms with the task of translating Brand*? I know that you worked from a literal translation by Inga-Stina Ewbank, but was it a play you already felt passionately about?*

No, I'd never read the play until I received the commission, but I then read it in a variety of translations. I must say that I came away from F. E. Garrett's old Everyman translation with considerable respect for it—although it's verse not poetry—and though the locutions of the verse are dated, I was impressed by his devotion to the text and his faithfulness to the metre and rhyming pattern of the play. I also read very widely in critical exegesis and opinion on the play. I became, almost against my will, fascinated not only by the daunting scale of the demand but also by my own deep and very mixed feelings about it. Both as a work of art and as a portrayal of a certain kind of character it contained a great deal that was hateful. I also became fascinated by certain technical matters. My attention was caught by a phrase of Ibsen's in which he said he wanted a metre in which he could career where he would 'as on horseback'. I enjoyed the challenge of having to move rapidly from farce to ecstasy.

Did you feel that you had to arrive at your own interpretation of the play?

No. If I do seem to have arrived at an 'interpretation' of the character it's probably an effect rather than a cause, a feedback from things I had to do at a technical level in order to make the poetry work. I tried to subject my idea of the character to Ibsen's, though I would fully accept that the Brand who moves in my version is not exactly the Brand who moves in Ibsen's. I did at one or two points slightly heighten the Kierkegaardian streak, and I know it's a highly debatable matter to what extent Ibsen was influenced, if at all, by Kierkegaard. I think he denied it himself, but notwithstanding his denial a number of scholars insist that he must have been. There is of course something crushing and appalling about the sheer bulk of the play.

You didn't feel you had to opt for taking Brand either as a man of genuine religious exaltation and messianic zeal or as a false messiah?

The interesting proposal that Ibsen seems to be putting forward is that it's possible at one and the same time to be a man of genuine zeal and messianic fervour, a life-defender, and a life-destroyer. I don't think Ibsen feels that the latter necessarily cancels out the former; in some quite dreadful way they co-exist. Ibsen gives us enough in the portrayal of surrounding characters like the Dean and the Mayor to make it perfectly understandable that a man like Brand should be filled with the kind of anger and indignation that he is. Given that canting, provincial, sanctimonious, murderously self-righteous society, a man like Brand is up to a point to be profoundly admired and understood. The tragedy is that that kind of absolute conviction, which is simultaneously a quite proper denunciation of the venial and mercenary world, is itself a murderous force.

What Ibsen presents in terms of that grotesque paradox is in one way quite consistent with the themes of your own work such as 'Funeral Music', don't you think?

Yes, with the benefit of hindsight, one can see now that *Brand* was not an inappropriate play for me to attempt. Certain things in the play are consistent with certain things that have held my interest in my other work, but I didn't approach the task with the kind of cool-headed logic that that would suggest. These are lines of connection we're only at liberty to discover now because in some miraculous way I managed to reverse the usual procedures of my work and to produce something like six thousand lines of verse in little more than a year.

Did you find it a liberating experience to have made a version of Brand *and did it teach you much?*

I thought at the time, in those last moments of exhausted euphoria, that it had taught me a great deal, that it had widened the scope of my art in a quite unexpected way, and that it had given me self-confidence and the means to write fluently. At the moment all that appears to have been an illusion, but it's not beyond the bounds of possibility that in ten years from now I may be working in a way that *Brand* prepared me for.

Going back to a more general question: do you actually practise any faith? Would you class yourself as an agnostic, or would you assent to Harold

Bloom's term 'desperate humanist'?

I would not wish to describe myself as an agnostic. There's a phrase by Joseph Cary in his book *Three Modern Italian Poets*[1]—I forget which poet he's referring to—that, if it were applied to my own poetry, might seem to be not wholly irrelevant, 'a heretic's dream of salvation expressed in the images of the orthodoxy from which he is excommunicate'. That seems to me an apt phrase to describe the area in which my poetry moves.

... although the word 'heretic' does imply a fairly deliberate and active posture ...

When I was writing 'Funeral Music', I was much interested in Averroism, which is, or was, a heresy, and for which I made a metaphor:

Averroes, old heathen,
If only you had been right, if Intellect
Itself were absolute law, sufficient grace,
Our lives could be a myth of captivity
Which we might enter: an unpeopled region
Of ever new-fallen snow, a palace blazing
With perpetual silence as with torches.

Averroism was the doctrine of monopsychism, that is, that there's only one single Intellect, or 'intellective' soul for the whole of humanity, and it seemed to me at first sight a most comforting doctrine—the idea that all kinds of personal guilt, a burden of culpability for all eternity, might be absorbed and absolved in that one 'Intellect'—but afterwards I felt it was not a doctrine to be embraced at all; it seemed to be the archetype of the totalitarian state. And so I reacted very violently against it, but for a time I had felt the attraction very strongly. The attraction of what I came to see as its specious comfort and also of its coldness is captured in that metaphor, which—if I can say so—managed to be quite beautiful while at the same time being an image of a beautiful coldness and desolation. What at first seemed comforting ended up being desolate, rather like one of those beautiful but terrifying fairy stories where one enters a

[1] New York University Press, 1969.

palace which is either totally empty or full of sleeping people, a dead sleep which is lit by blazing torches, never replenished and yet never extinguished.

'Heretic', as you say, does imply a conscious act of defiance and choice, and what one is really describing is a sense of exclusion, of excommunication. Excommunication is a more passive thing than a heresy is.

One of your critics has written, 'Hill binds the meditativeness of his poetry fiercely to action in a wordly sense',[1] *which perhaps suggests more of a polemical stance than you would allow? It implies that poetry should have issue in more responsible behaviour, don't you think?*

Poetry is responsible. It's a form of responsible behaviour, not a directive. It is an exemplary exercise. Ezra Pound said in his *Letters* that 'The poet's job is to define and yet again define, till the detail of surface is in accord with the root in justice.'[2]

[1] Merle Brown, 'Geoffrey Hill's "Funeral Music"', *Agenda* (Geoffrey Hill Special Issue), vol. 17 no. 1, Spring 1979, p. 87.

[2] D. D. Paige (ed.), *The Letters of Ezra Pound*, Faber, 1951, p. 366.

THOMAS KINSELLA

Were you born in Dublin?

Yes, born in Dublin in 1928, and raised in a little village near Chapelizod. My father and mother were both from the Liberties area of Dublin, and my grandparents were there, so I grew up knowing a very central part of Dublin—Bow Lane, Basin Lane, the end of the Canal—and aware also of where my grandparents had come from: in one case, south Wicklow, in the other, near Mullingar. I have a fairly complicated sense of Irish origins mixed up with my own first memories of life on a fringe of Dublin, an almost rural village. My father and his father before him worked in Guinness's: my grandfather ran one of the barges from the brewery jetty to the sea-going vessels in the harbour; my father worked in the cooperage.

Was the Catholicism of your upbringing a strong influence upon you?

It was so pervasive that it hardly counted as an influence at all; it was a reality like oxygen.

And there was no question of your questioning it at that time?

Not at that time. Not that it ever became a great issue—a kind of general indifference arose and overwhelmed it. It disappeared more or less without fuss over a longish period.

Do you ever regret that movement, as it were, away from the underpinning of your childhood?

No, the supports that one might think of finding in organized religion I found elsewhere. It was a matter of clearing the decks rather than of losing something. The elaborately prepared solutions of Catholicism worked for a long while, but it was no great loss when I found myself without them.

Did your parents influence you greatly?

My father was a great reader, a very concerned person. He was a member of the Left Book Club, and had all the lively books of the thirties. It would certainly be impossible in his company to miss what was going on, that a world war was developing and that social issues of various calibres were involved.

Did you read English at University College, Dublin?

I started in Economics. My career took me from school into the Civil Service. I studied English for a short while, but economics and politics were my main interests. I began writing poems at the same time, and became committed very fast. The things behind form were what bothered me, having to do with content, exploratory form—the sequence rather than the finished single object.

What sort of person are you? You've written that you're drawn to both rigour and squalor, and a certain bitterness figures in your work . . .

I'd be no stranger to a certain flexible sloppiness, but the rigour is what's important: I believe the significant work begins in eliciting order from actuality. We're surrounded and penetrated by squalor, disorder and the insignificant, and I believe the artistic impulse has a great deal to do with our trying to make sense out of that.

Your earliest poems quite obviously take the influence of Auden and Yeats.

Yes, the earliest poems that I still think are good were written quite specifically in Auden's manner: 'A Lady of Quality' is specifically modelled, as an exercise, on a poem of Auden's. My early writing was completely exploratory, aimed partly at finding my own voice. At a certain stage I found myself writing a book of poems, rather than merely collecting poems into a book.

In 1966 you wrote that your poetry of the last decade had 'dealt with love, death and the artistic act; with persons and relationships, places and objects, seen against the world's processes of growth, maturing and extinction'. Would you now update those remarks? What emphases and procedures have changed or developed in your work?

It sounds very large-mouthed . . . But I think that's still what I'm doing. Though I've tried to find larger, sequential forms—

open-ended—so that the effort can continue inside a more stable continuum.

Similarly, in 1967, you wrote about the poems in Nightwalker *that 'their subject in general is a developing view of life as an ordeal.' Can you perhaps explain what brought you to that view?*

I see it now as just one of the given things: one is presented with a lifespan which manifests itself largely as ordeal, stages through which one is tested more and more deeply. An awareness of life as ordeal will lead inevitably, in a certain temperament, to an artistic response, an attempt to hold things in place.

I think there's an essential paradox in your view, isn't there, in that despite what you've often called our 'hunger' for order and understanding, we can never achieve it? Do you feel that you've grown nearer to coping with that dilemma in your work of the last ten years?

Yes, and almost to admiring the system itself. Though one fails at these exercises, one still hands the exercise on. It's a marvellous and fruitful system, never repeating itself.

Would you be happy to call yourself a moralist, or perhaps a spoiled romantic?

Maybe a spoiled romantic, but neither term would suffice. Responsibility is a term I would use, responsibility toward actuality. I think of the word responsibility in reaction against your word 'moral'.

If you've experienced a deep sense of dislocation and depredation in life, do you feel that your poetry should speak for a general cultural dislocation as much as for the personal impulse?

I'd like to change the terms of what you say: despite the fact that the system has so many negative aspects, it also offers positive features, like love, continuity and amplification. Even though it may result in depredation and extinction, the positive characteristics are what keep me interested.

But it seems to me that in your work there's a predominant sense almost of determinism?

That may well be so up to now, but I don't feel like that any more. Mellower . . . For instance, the poetry I've most recently finished is part of a continuing investigation into the given human beings in my past—parents and grandparents—who seem to me very valuable instances, and to have undergone some very positive as well as negative experiences. The poetry is growing, I think, in response to these things. The positive aspect that interests me now is only latent in my earlier things, which do to some extent dwell on mutilation and the negative . . .

Many of your poems do draw towards the sense of affirmation you're talking about, a sense of affirmation and grace in terms, for example, of a belief in personal love. Yet the burden of those same poems is often enough a rumination on dispossession and grief. Do you now feel that poems like 'Phoenix Park' were a kind of whistling in the dark? In other words, were you in a way betraying your severe and dark apprehensions of the mess of Irish life by overlaying them with good intentions (I'm thinking of Eliot's remark about compromising reality with 'unattained aspirations')?

I'd certainly never dream of pushing it as far as any kind of unreasonable hope, but I would be quite content to rest in the potentiality, the possibility, of an order inherent in experience—however dark.

Would you feel that your poems rely more on a fidelity to experience or on speculative truth?

They lean toward the accurate perception of reality, away from speculation. I would feel more uneasy now in a metaphysical scheme than I would have years ago. I would rather settle for the facts and let them speak among themselves.

Is there a philosophical or religious pattern you can see?

None that still survives. No fixed body of thought or belief could survive the processes I have been through in the last ten to fifteen years.

Do you think your earlier work is best described as diagnostic?

The very early poems possibly—by borrowed impulse from some of Yeats's middle poetry and from Auden. But my poetry has been losing its metaphysical content very fast.

What was so attractive to you in Yeats or Auden?

'But Love has pitched its mansion in/the place of excrement', in Yeats's case. Or Auden's grace under pressure (I mean his capacity to emerge throughout his career, whatever the pressure, with a poem of grace, beauty, charm, seductive rhythm—all those superficial things). It would be a little later that I would find much more satisfaction in the forms of Ezra Pound's *Cantos*. Finally, I don't think graceful postures are adequate; you have to deal with the raw material.

Can you say why, in a good many poems, you've opted for generalization and allegory rather than for specific and literal occasions?

Maybe that's something I'm trying to forget. I think at the beginning my poems were influenced by literature more than by fact. I would regard the direct dealing with matter as something that requires great sophistication and equipment.

In poems such as 'Baggot Street Deserta', 'Downstream' and 'Nightwalker' you adopted a figure in allegorical movement, tracing an inductive path through experience.

The obsession with fact, with specific individual data, wouldn't seem to me to make much sense unless it had some allegorical drive behind it. Experience by itself, however significant, won't do.

Maurice Harmon has written that your 'technical problem is to project this vision of inherent and inescapable evil and to convey at the same time his sense of those orderly and acceptable relationships which he detected'.[1] *Is that the truth of your task?*

There's an over-emphasis there on the matter of evil. It's potentially negative—there's a darkness in the whole exercise—but the *structure* militates against that: it counteracts the evil. However, I don't believe I have a defined position which I must defend or be prepared to surrender. One can adopt a posture which proves enabling for a long time, but I'd hang my hat on the recognition, or the hope, that larger forms and states of order can emerge from larger bodies of experience. Hopefully, my poems are fitting into a larger whole in which they'll have larger and more organically related meanings (although some of the poems that have given me most pleasure are occasional poems, poems such as 'The Good Fight' and 'Dick King', and some of the poems in the sequence 'One'). Some of the poems that I'm most committed to are in *Notes from the Land of the Dead*—poems about the grandmother—and those are completely exploratory still.

[1] *The Poetry of Thomas Kinsella*, Wolfhound Press, Dublin, 1974, p. 35.

In the simple and affecting poem 'Tear' from that sequence, you used a loose stanzaic structure . . .

Yes, it's a poem that's very closely related to another of the sequence, 'Ancestor', but it's quite instinctive and is certainly a poem that doesn't close and still has the potential for development.

A number of critics describe your poems as reveries or meditations, which perhaps implies quietude or the pacific, and yet it seems to me that a fair number of them are kinetic, active and angry, and express strong convictions.

I would see them as set pieces—'Downstream', for instance—with the poetic impulse having to do with the realization of structure; but the poem wouldn't have been written in pursuit of this idea. I hope the echoes of one poem or sequence go on and get caught by the next. The poems I'm writing now will, I hope, gather up previous work as well as move forward.

Would you acknowledge the idea that your poetry has a mystical element?

Shyly . . . I would deny a normal religious element, but the poems *are* larger than life, with order and a profounder meaning.

Can you explain what you meant when you said in a Radio Eireann 1974 broadcast, 'Ireland is a necessary burden, a place I must keep coming back to, I must keep trying to understand. It gets less and less rewarding, but it becomes more and more necessary.'?

I detect the voice of an exile there, a certain hysteria. But I've arranged to spend a great deal of time in Ireland since then and no longer have that sense of it. I'm attached to Temple University in Philadelphia and spend eight months a year in Dublin, on the basis of a course I developed on the Irish tradition for American students, who settle for a semester of study in Dublin. I myself derive increased understanding from the brilliant teaching and work of many friends. I believe I might have festered and gone sterile if we hadn't managed to come back to Dublin.

John Montague felt that what he detected as a Parnassian quality in your early work might benefit from the more experimental poetic climate of America. Do you feel that you've profited from an Hiberno–American cross-fertilization?

I'm certainly grateful to the work of Ezra Pound and William Carlos Williams for having opened up particular lines of style—not by any means for imitation, but revelations of scope and attitude—and (particularly in Williams's case) of a kind of creative relaxation in the face of complex reality; to remain open, 'prehensile', not rigidly committed. It's a matter of staying agile so that one's poetic organism can respond fully. The response becomes one's life-work, rather than a sequence of individual poems.

Would you agree with Maurice Harmon's view that Nightwalker *'on the whole is less concerned with general manifestations of nightmarish evil than with immediate experiences of pain'?*[1]

The poem does focus directly on certain painful affairs, but I doubt it is merely a record of a particular painful progress—though the tendency to generalize is weakening... One gets more and more hesitant; I wouldn't presume now to sum up a state of affairs as, for instance, moral or proper. I don't believe the creative response has anything to do with making people behave better, it has to do with understanding them—however they behave.

In 'Nightwalker' there seems to be a certain amount of sarcasm, if I can call it that, at the expense of Irish Nationalism or the mercantile compromises Ireland was making at the time ...

Those were easy targets. I would step back and let the opinions of the main character emerge without feeling committed to them as a writer, even though he is of course oneself. The creative response separates itself even to the actual protagonist, who happens to be oneself; another aspect of consciousness deals in the creative understanding of this self who is dramatically captured.

Are you speaking of an ironic tactic?

It wouldn't be irony, but a distancing of the self. It would have designs but be innocent and direct, a purification of attitude. I would reserve a different stance for occasional poetry such as 'Butcher's Dozen', where I would feel free to lay about me in my own voice.

[1] Ibid., p. 51.

Is it too strong to see a tragic sense of life in your early poems, even perhaps a nihilistic one?

No: I might have to agree with that.

I mean that however much the poet, in Frost's phrase, cries out upon life with a feeling of persistence and the quality of the poetic act, his assertions are disabused by the knowledge of failure and death.

Yes, except that I would put increasing force behind the actuality of the response. If an artistic response is called into existence, that itself modifies the situation: it's a positive response even if we never solve anything. It colours reality in a way that makes it more acceptable.

Do you feel that you've moved into an area of wise passiveness in the later work?

I would like to believe that. I'm certainly not committed to a set of negatives or to crying out against the ordeal of life. What you might call the ethic of suffering has gone into the past. The artistic impulse justifies reality and man's part in it; the human race makes sense of its fix.

The early work does seem to show a deliberate and determined stance of commitment towards suffering and bitterness. Were you regretful of the willed rhetoric you employed, for instance, in parts of 'Nightwalker'?

The thing I'd recognize *now* and see as a flaw, is that it *was* possible to be a victim of that kind of rhetoric. I couldn't ever again go in for that sort of full-throated outcry. What seems much more interesting now is the kind of actuality that gets into a poem like 'Tear': a mute communication between a child and an ancient woman.

The last stanza is a specific memory,

> *How long and hard it is*
> *before you get to Heaven,*
> *unless like little Agnes*
> *you vanish with early tears.*

—which of course leaves the question in suspension?

Yes, a refusal to permit the poem to fulfil its own form; it's a loose end dramatically, implying what hasn't been included, keeping it valid for later use. It leaves an available hook.

Could you explain how the poem called 'Sacrifice' finds its place in the sequence of 'a single drop'?

It's an act of sacrifice seen allegorically as the offering of one's heart to another; it earns its place because the distance between narrator and protagonist has become enormous. Getting 'Sacrifice' to operate within an apparently personal sequence had to be achieved stage by stage. The rest of the sequence pursues it.

Did you make a conscious decision to renounce received forms and rhyme?

Yes, I kicked the whole scheme asunder at a certain point, realizing that the modern poet has inherited wonderfully enabling free forms. My poems have a form which ought to be felt as a whole, rather than in, e.g., stanzaic expectations. Each poem has a unique shape, contents and development. The 'nightnothing' sequence, for example, develops by splaying out in all directions. I can 'inhabit' the protagonist of a poem like 'Good Night' without feeling committed as a narrator to end the poem at a particular point.

Would it alarm you if a critic interpreted a poem in a way you hadn't designed?

It would, although I'd be prepared for a lot of open manoeuvering. I don't recall any bad 'mistakes' by the critics, but I believe there is a great deal more in the work than has been seen. In *Notes from the Land of the Dead*, for instance, there are two poems employing the characters of an old lady and a young boy, in one of which—'The High Road'—she gives him a gift—a little toy, the mandoline—which is sterile, while in the other, 'A Hand of Solo', he is given a gift which he negotiates with her—and it is fertile, it *works*. There's an implied gamut of activity and response in the two acts, a largeness of experience embodied—to my satisfaction at least—in the two gestures.

In 'A Hand of Solo' the fact that he buys a pomegranate with a penny is mere fact, and yet there is a great boldness of meaning in the pomegranate being in fact the fruit of life and death: it is full of seed and blood, and both of those aspects are taken care of in the poem. I was electrified and thrilled that after putting so much weight of memory on the pomegranate it also responded mythologically. But I would settle for the 'random pursuit' of a poem rather than labour to produce something coherent and recognizable and traditional. If the pomegranate had been a less allegorical fruit, that would have been quite all right.

Do you feel your work has striven more and more towards a myth of the imagination?

If it does, that's a bonus: I don't aim at it. But that is probably what happens when you have the impulse merely to understand, not to impose order.

I think many critics regard it as a bad procedure to depart from specific real contexts in order to divagate upon a certain metaphysical dreaminess, but you'd presumably set more store by allegory?

I would obey the facts—as in not calling the fruit a pomegranate unless it had been one. Insofar as the poems enshrine specific references, the references would be exact.

It seems to me that for a great stretch of your work the passion would be one of frustration, almost of exacerbation.

Yes, but it doesn't feel so bad any more! I don't feel so victimized and trapped now. Perhaps nicer things are happening to me—or maybe the act of understanding gives one a larger attitude.

I want to ask you about one early poem, 'The Monk', which—according to Maurice Harmon—takes 'delight in death',[1] *while it seems to me more to do with a dream of beauty which is devoured by the waking world.*

It's again an exercise in inhabiting the persona, who is scrubbing and chillily preparing himself. To put it crudely, the monk is envisaging heaven, but I as narrator wouldn't have any commitment to his attitude.

Dreams figure largely in your poetry, dreams perhaps of ideal order which are immediately subjected to the limitations of actuality, and it's presumably fair for me to infer that you are not an idealist?

Yes, I wouldn't feel committed by any aspect of the ideal—or moral. It's possible to commit oneself totally in an exploratory way, as one might in parts of 'Downstream', and then start again completely uncommitted. One changes, develops, and abandons positions.

Is that to say that your personal views, whether political or social, don't

[1] Ibid., p. 23.

enter the poems in a way that should be identified?

If they do, they are 'dramatically' presented. But with occasional poems like 'The Good Fight' the rules change: some of the statements in that poem are as near directly moral as I've ever got.

Can you say where your attitude figures most strongly in 'The Good Fight', which seems overall to be concerned with a debate between Platonic idealism and contingent reality?

Apart from the dramatic ending, there is a voice in Section I commenting directly on certain political attitudes:

> (It sounds as though it could go on for ever,
> yet there is a shape to it—Appropriate
> Performance. Another almost perfect
> working model . . . But it gets harder,
> The concepts jerk and wrestle, back to back.
> The finer the idea the harder it is
> to assemble lifelike. It adopts hardnesses
> and inflexibilities, knots, impossible joints
> made possible only by stress,
> and good for very little afterward.)

The tone at the end of that section is sardonic and meant to be dismissive:

> Inside, a group of specialists,
> chosen for their incomparable dash,
> were gathered around
> a map of the world's regions
> with all kinds of precision instruments.

There is a very close relationship between the 'I' as narrator and the 'I' as protagonist in the sick second section, where the assassin is preparing his state of mind. There would be a case for finding the same sort of attitude in the creative response as there is in this assassin's response, where he likens himself to a shark who can't stop, who must keep moving through his element; the moment he relaxes, he drowns. So there are commitments of a kind there. And also at the end, when the Robert Frost character is made to totter out and embody certain statements—those are statements one could feel committed to still:

> it is we, letting things *be*,
> who might come at understanding.

I got a good deal of it said in that section.

Can you say what facet or attitude you still feel committed to in 'Nightwalker'—perhaps the view that we owe a debt to the past, and yet the past shadows the present as a burden?

The third section opens with what has developed since I wrote the poem as a whole:

> I believe now that love is half persistence,
> A medium in which, from change to change,
> Understanding may be gathered.

The only thing that one can feel committed to is the whole process of change and the possibility of understanding, as long as your organs of perception and understanding remain functioning. I would find that it counterbalances any notion of nihilism. The impulse is important, even if it's of no avail, and I finally got that said in one of the Peppercanister poems.

The 'Epilogue' to the sequence 'One' seems to point back to the isolation of the individual, the solitude of the endeavour . . .

It's true for that phase, and it's associated with the numeral 1 which is being deliberately explored at that point. In *Notes from the Land of the Dead*, the O manifested itself half-way through the book, but the patron numeral was clearly established in 'One', and—for what it's worth—the next book hovers on the notion of two, the divided unit.

The twenty-four sections of 'A Technical Supplement' cover an enormous range, as it were anatomizing the nature of being. Did you see it in terms of a search for identity?

It's a plunge of a different kind into the nature of things—how objectionable and how pleasant, how rewarding and how diabolical—without being committed to any particular point of view except that of dynamic response to whatever happens.

It's a difficult poem for the reader in that it has no narrative line.

It proceeds through a less organized or less limited sequence of states of mind, and works itself out quite programmatically: in fact, the last section is a continuation of the plot through the larger sequence from *Notes from the Land of the Dead* into my recent work.

What do you mean by plot?

The running effect of this numerological system. I'm talking about tactics rather than the nature of the subject matter. The number 1 doesn't offend the subjects of that sequence called 'One' in concentrating on its unitary—backbone, or male—aspects. At the end of 'His Father's Hands', the breaking-up of the unit, the block of wood, is sexual:

> it turned under my hands, an axis
> of light flashing down its length,
> and the wood's soft flesh broke open,
> countless little nails
> squirming and dropping out of it

and the thing becomes saturated with potential: there's the allegorical level of the datum. And the block did exactly that as far as actuality is concerned—not that it matters, except to me.

Why did you find it important and necessary to undertake the immense work of translating The Tain?

It's an act of responsibility. It's ours, Irish, and it deserved a new currency; and the same is true of the representative selection that Seán Ó Tuama and I are now working on—from 1600 to 1900—and I'm also translating some from the Middle Irish. It's a commitment to tradition; an understanding of them, as part of *our* past, is an understanding of our totality. It's also the very best way I know of appreciating the work itself. *The Tain* is part of our imaginative bedrock, and my translation was an act of loyalty to that part of one's own past, not necessarily to the quality of that particular work.

Do you feel a kinship with other contemporary poets?

The simple answer is: No. I don't feel that there is a group activity afoot in which I play a part, or a creative heave in which maybe two or three poets are engaged. I don't think it's as coherent as it looks: it would be pure journalism to think like that.

How would you sum up your view of the function of poetry?

For the moment it would appear to me that the artistic act has to do with the eliciting of order from significant experience, so as to come to terms with that experience on the basis of understanding of some kind. That all sounds very circular, but it's a tying-up of the impulse into the act itself. Whether or not that involves any didactic outcome depends on the individual age, but in fact it's not central, it doesn't matter. Understanding experience presupposes taking it on exactly its own terms. A good work of art embodies the capacity to grow, to keep the potential for enlarged relevance: it never goes out of date, it's as alive as any organic thing. Images and symbols are a way of embodying the kinetic in the static: it's a mystery, but it happens. If adequately understood and responded to, poetry should add dynamically to the understanding of the reader. It is a form of significant reality processed in advance for the understanding; it's like a meaningful model for the life lived. I try to use the word 'significant' only to mean that which will bother all of us equally.

PHILIP LARKIN

You once wrote that if you were to try your hand at autobiography you'd have to begin at the age of twenty-one, or even thirty-one . . .

Yes. Next question? (*Laughs*) Whenever I read an autobiography, or even a biography, I tend to start half-way through, where the chap's grown-up and it becomes interesting. Some writers seem to stop at twenty-one rather than start there: Betjeman, Day Lewis. Still, there's probably a good physiological reason for this: old people remember what happened forty years ago but not last week. Goethe says somewhere that what is distant seems to him immediate, and vice versa. No doubt when I get to my dotage all those dusty motor-car-filled days in Coventry will seem vivid and delightful, but just now they're far away. My childhood wasn't unhappy, just boring.

Does your feeling imply a regret that you can't attach more significance to your childhood—no traumas, no villainous mother?

Well, it would have been nice to have more technicolor, so to speak.

You've reviewed a number of biographies—Christina Rossetti, for example, Owen and Housman—and have always held that it's some sort of aberration to take childhood, in the way of Walter de la Mare, as the great beneficent lap of the world.

I think it is. If you're more interesting as a child than as a grown-up, what's the point of growing up? I think grown-ups are nicer than children. I hated everybody when I was a child, or I thought I did. When I grew up, I realized that what I hated was children.

You've written that children have been devalued—we don't think of them any more as holy innocents . . .

I think that since the middle class was reintroduced to its offspring by the disappearance of servants a good many people feel this. Of course I speak as a childless person: I've never lived in hideous contact with them, having toast flung about at breakfast and so on. Perhaps worse than toast. The whole doctrine of original sin implies that children are awful, don't you think? The nearer you are to being born, the worse you are. I wasn't a happy child: I stammered badly, and this tends to shape your life. You can't become a lecturer or anything that involves talking. By the time you cure yourself—which in my case was quite late, about thirty—all the talking things you might have done are lost. If you catch me tired or frightened, I still stammer.

Was that why you became a librarian?

I tried twice for the Civil Service, during the war of course, but even in those days they had some standards. I'm glad now that they didn't take me, though I was a bit surprised then. I've been much happier as a librarian.

Did you find Oxford a nourishing experience? You did make some close friends there, such as Kingsley Amis.

I made some very good friends and enjoyed being there, but I never had the *Brideshead Revisited* feeling about it. I could never write there. Although I love the place, I feel a pressure at the back of my neck at being surrounded by about six thousand people who are cleverer than I am. When I left I felt a great upsurge of—well, since it's so long ago I'll call it creative relief. I wrote *The North Ship*, *Jill* and *A Girl in Winter* in about two years, straight off.

Was Jill *in fact close to your own experience, and if so does it now embarrass you?*

It embarrasses me a bit by being so very much a first novel, but apart from the air-raid—that was Coventry in November 1940, just after I'd gone to Oxford—it's not my own experience. I shared rooms with an old school friend, and had plenty of good times. I certainly didn't have any fantasies about a schoolgirl sister. But at the same time a lot of it is what I felt. The incidental details are mostly imaginary, but the feeling is absolutely true.

And yet the book explores a mentality that is uncomfortable there.

It's all rather paradoxical really. John Kemp is uncomfortable because he's working class, but I made him working class to give him some inadequacy, some equivalent of my stammer. I was sort of professional middle class. *Jill* has always had the edge over *A Girl in Winter* as far as sales go, which surprises me because that's a much more sophisticated book—written, shaped, a Virginia Woolf–Henry Green kind of novel. I took much more trouble over it. But I don't think either of them is any good.

You've said somewhere that, in your view, novelists are interested in other people, but you're not . . .

I don't think my books were novels, they were more kinds of prose poems. I spent about five years trying to write a third novel, but couldn't. When I lapsed back into poetry, it was so much easier, so much quicker. It's not characters that are the trouble in writing a novel, it's finding a background for them, knowing what they do.

In reviewing biographies of writers, you've taken pains to analyse what gives each one his or her particular emphasis, what provokes their work, and to define any crisis or shift in their lives as if it were a cause of their writing. That's to say, your reviews tend towards a biographical interpretation of a writer's work . . .

I think we *want* the life and the work to make sense together: I suppose ultimately they must, since they both relate to the same person. Eliot would say they don't, but I think Eliot is wrong.

I think you've said that a writer must write the truth—presumably the truth of his experience?

I was probably lying. A more important thing I said was that every poem starts out as either true or beautiful. Then you try to make the true ones seem beautiful, and the beautiful ones true. I could go through my poems marking them as one or the other. 'Send No Money' is true. 'Essential Beauty' is beautiful. When I say beautiful, I mean the original idea seemed beautiful. When I say true, I mean something was grinding its knuckles in my neck and I thought: God, I've got to say this somehow, I have to find words and I'll make them as beautiful as possible. 'Dockery and

Son': that's a true one. It's never reprinted in anthologies, but it's as true as anything I've ever written—for me anyway.

At the end of that poem you have what amounts to a statement:

> *Life is first boredom, then fear.*
> *Whether or not we use it, it goes,*
> *And leaves what something hidden from us chose,*
> *And age, and then the only end of age.*

Do you think that sort of enunciation is imaginatively justified within the poem, or did you feel it true-as-true?

Both. I'm very proud of those lines. They're true. I remember when I was writing it, I thought this is how it's got to end. There's a break in the metre; it's meant as a jolt.

A number of critics have commented on the fact that, even as early as The North Ship, *you seem to have decided that life is a matter of regretfulness, of unfulfilment. Many of the poems in the book are kinds of lucubration, thoughts on love, and the paradox whereby one only values something when it's past . . .*

I can't really go back to *The North Ship*: it was so very young, born of reading Yeats and so on. Remember Yeats's early poems were wan and droopy, very unlike the later Yeats. I can't explain *The North Ship* at all. It's not very good, though your courtesy will prevent you from agreeing. It's popular with musicians, they like setting it. Musicians like things that don't mean too much.

But there is meaning in the book.

Do you think so? I have to make a tape-recording for America, and I'm putting in three *North Ship* poems—'X', 'XIII' and 'XXX'—only because I think they're fairly acceptable as poems: they're not meant to be what I think good nowadays. I don't particularly like 'XXX' except for the last quatrain. There are some pieces in the book I hate very much indeed.

I quite like number XXV.

It's not very sharp, is it? I distinctly remember the dream and what it was about, but it's quite unimportant.

Do you believe that the poet can best explain his own work?

As to what it was about or what it's supposed to mean, yes, not as to whether it's any good.

But what if a critic construes a poem in a way you felt you didn't mean?

I should think he was talking balls. I get endless trouble about 'Dry-Point'. Schoolgirls write to me about it, and I have to explain that originally it was one of two poems about sex, and that modesty forbids me to say any more. They were written in the late forties: Kingsley called the first one my Sanders of the River poem—that was the first one, whooping it up—and I was so dashed that I dropped it. 'Dry-point' is the other, saying how awful sex is and how we want to get away from it.

Do you still feel, as you told Ian Hamilton many years ago, that critics can hinder your work?

Yes. A critic can never help you. He can say you should be writing like someone else, which is like water off a duck's back. But if he says, 'Larkin, you're crumby, anti-life, defeatist' and so on, you may get so depressed that you pack it up—if you read him, that is.

You think of yourself as an emotional poet, and it must strike you as ironic when some critics describe you as 'neutral', especially when you've spoken of some poems as being almost shamefully self-revealing?

Well, there are many types of emotion. I've said that depression is to me as daffodils were to Wordsworth. But a poem isn't only emotion. In my experience you've got the emotion side—let's call it the fork side—and you cross it with the knife side, the side that wants to sort it out, chop it up, arrange it, and say either thank you for it or sod the universe for it. You never write a poem out of emotion alone, just as you never write a poem from the knife side, what might be a letter to *The Times*. I can't explain it: don't want to.

Can we speak a little about your response to Hardy? You remarked in one review about Hardy's sense of time as being a necessary ingredient of spiritual growth . . .

This goes back to what we were saying about children, doesn't it, who know nothing about life. I think that until you're about thirty you really haven't got things into perspective: the term 'young poet' seems a contradiction in terms to me.

If one extends what you're saying to the practice of writing poetry, what do you say to your critics who imply or infer that at some point you predeter-

mined what you felt about life, that you made up your mind once and for all, for example, about the occasions of suffering that people endure?

They've got it the wrong way round. I don't decide what I think about life: life decides that, either through heredity or environment, what you're born with or what happens to you. If I'd been born a different person and different things had happened to me, I might have written differently. I didn't invent age and death and failure and all that, but how can you ignore them? Hardy or someone said that life was a comedy to those who think, but a tragedy to those who feel. Good stuff.

Do you actually share Hardy's feeling for what you've called the 'passive apprehension of suffering' and the capacity for spiritual growth it can bring?

The more sensitive you are to suffering the nicer person you are and the more accurate notion of life you have. Hardy had it right from the start: his early poems are wonderful—'She, to Him', for example. As I tried to say in 'Deceptions', the inflicter of suffering may be fooled, but the sufferer never is.

I suppose what I'm asking is why you've felt that suffering is the real thing in life, and haven't expressed more of what other people find fulfilling?

I just think it is. The really happy moments of my life, such as when I caught the captain of the other side in the deep or passed my driving test first go, aren't really subjects for poetry. And they don't stay with you.

Do you feel that you've carried out Wordsworth's dictum that a great poet must create the taste by which he is to be enjoyed and understood?

Please don't think that I'm great. If I'm noticeable, it's because we're in a trough at the moment. Forty years ago we had Yeats, Eliot, Graves, Auden, Spender, MacNeice, Betjeman, Dylan Thomas; and who have we got now? If I seem good, it's because everyone else is so bad. Well, almost everyone. Well, anyway . . .

You don't think of yourself as didactic at all?

Not really. One of the minor mistakes people make about me is thinking that I'm a sort of cut-price Betjeman. Now he *is* didactic: a real protest poet—'Come, friendly bombs, and fall on Slough' and that kind of thing. He's always against uglification, greed, vulgarity and the rest of it. I just accept them for the most part.

You've observed in writing that 'poetry is an affair of sanity', which does seem to imply the view that it must be level-headed, can't admit anything that doesn't seem tolerable and can't tax the reader ... but perhaps you made the remark against experimentalism or the oddness you found in Emily Dickinson?

There certainly is a cult of the mad these days: think of all the boys who've been in the bin—I don't understand it. Chaucer, Shakespeare, Wordsworth, Hardy—it's the big, sane boys who get the medals. The object of writing is to show life as it is, and if you don't see it like that you're in trouble, not life. Up to you, of course.

What answer do you make to those who find your work defeatist?

I don't find anything defeatist about being sane, do you? I know Lawrence said tragedy ought to be a great big kick at misery, but then Lawrence was Lawrence, a man I've always admired. I love *Lady Chatterley's Lover*, just because it doesn't come to a happy ending, or any sort of ending: Mellors is like everyone else, he wants to have his end away and then forget about it. It's a very equivocal ending.

Isn't there a danger in adducing one's own temperament as the truth about life?

A danger who for? Nobody pays any attention to what you write. They read it and then forget about it. There may be a lunatic fringe who believe that life is what writers say, not what they experience themselves, but most people just say, 'Oh well, that's what it's like to be Larkin', and start thinking about something else.

And yet, to go back to the sort of statement you make at the end of 'Dockery and Son': you see it as true, but others might dispute it.

It's a bit simplified, I suppose, but I think it's all perfectly true. I can't see how anyone could possibly deny it, any of it.

If I can raise one further criticism: Raymond Gardiner wrote in 1973 that 'Philip Larkin's poetry represents an art of desolation ... it lacks the humanity of comfort ...'[1] *I've rather unfairly extrapolated from his com-*

[1] *Guardian*, 31 March 1973, p. 12.

ments, but can you bear such appraisals or do they provoke you?

The drift of these questions seems to be that I shouldn't be myself, I should be somebody else. Well, there may be something to be said for that, but it's not a thing I can do anything about. I don't want to turn other people into me, I'm only saying what I feel. It's very difficult to write about happiness. 'Happiness writes white,' as Montherlant says somewhere: in other words, you can't read it afterwards. It would be fun to be a novelist and write about imaginary happiness: I suppose lots of people do. Wonderful weathers and landscapes, and a new girl in every chapter.

I want to ask you why you resist going abroad. Betjeman said that he feels frustrated by his ignorance in foreign countries, but that's something different from what you said in your speech to the FVS Foundation in Hamburg when you won the Shakespeare Prize in 1977—that a poet who goes from country to country might find that 'his sense of cultural identity becomes blurred and weakened.'

Perhaps I was unlucky. My father liked going to Germany, and took me twice, when I was fourteen or so. I found it petrifying, not being able to speak to anyone or read anything, frightening notices that you felt you should understand and couldn't. My father liked the jolly singing in beer-cellars, three-four time to accordions—SchifferKlavier, did they call them?—think of that for someone who was just buying the first Count Basie records! Perhaps if I'd been younger, or older, or with people my own age even, it would have been different, but I doubt it. It's a language thing with me: I can't learn foreign languages, I just don't believe in them. As for cultural identities, that sounds a bit pretentious, but I think people do get pallid if they change countries. Look at Auden. But people must suit themselves.

But it might be said that in not exposing yourself to European cultures or literature, you're possibly cultivating a sort of narrow-mindedness or chauvinism . . .

But honestly, how far can one really assimilate literature in another language? In the sense that you can read your own?

Yet, by not trying, one might be courting a social, personal or national security, an insularity . . .

I don't think poetry is like that. Poems don't come from other poems, they come from being oneself, in life. Every man is an island, entire of himself, as Donne said. This American idea—it is American, isn't it? Started with Pound and Eliot?—that somehow every new poem has to be the sum of all old poems, like the latest Ford, well, it's the sort of idea lecturers get, if you'll excuse my saying so. Makes sense and so on: only it's not how poetry works. You remember that wonderful remark of Sidney Bechet when the recording engineer asked if he'd like to hear a playback: 'That don't do me no good.' That's what I think about foreign literature.

Would you actually accept Donald Davie's view of your philosophy of life as being 'patiently diminished'?

Funny sort of phrase. I don't think I understand it. I didn't invent old age and death and failure and disillusion: they're there, and I don't see why I shouldn't write about them if they seem writeable-about. No, it all comes down to what I said before: people don't want you to be yourself. It's really not so very far from being told, 'Now, comrade, let's have a poem about this month's steel production. None of this bourgeois personalism, unless you want to see the inside of Downing College.' You write a poem because it's something you've got to get done, not because it's a philosophy of life.

Do you take great care in ordering the poems in a collection?

Yes, great care. I treat them like a music-hall bill: you know, contrast, difference in length, the comic, the Irish tenor, bring on the girls. I think 'Lines on a Young Lady's Photograph Album' is a good opener, for instance; easy to understand, variety of mood, pretty end. The last one is chosen for its uplift quality, to leave the impression that you're more serious than the reader had thought.

Within The Less Deceived *you have a group of three poems basically about mortality—'Next, Please', 'Going' and 'Wants'—before providing a counter-movement in 'Maiden Name', which is about a sense of preservation from time . . .*

I used to be quite original in those days. As far as I know, nobody else has written about maiden names, and yet they are very powerful things. I often wonder how women survive the transition: if you're called something, you can't be called something else. Like I was saying about foreign languages.

I wonder if you could say something about a poem I like called 'If, My Darling', or perhaps somebody's asked you that before?

Never, nobody's paid the slightest attention to it. I like it very much too. It was the first poem that made Kingsley think I was some good: he loved it when I sent it to him. I wanted, in the last line, to change 'unpriceable' to 'unprintable', but he said no: 'unprintable' would just mean cunt, whereas 'unpriceable' *probably* meant cunt but could mean all sorts of other things too.

It's a fantastically self-derogatory poem, telling the girl that if she really knew me she'd know what a terrible person I am . . .

Well, I think we all think that, with girls. It's funny rather than self-derogatory. I'm surprised it hasn't been anthologized more.

Do you value as highly a poem such as 'Spring', another one in which you look at yourself deprecatingly, but with a difference in tone?

I don't think that's a particularly good poem, though there are some nice things in it. I like the last few lines.

The mood certainly takes off in those lines, but perhaps you can explain your feeling about the last passage;

> *And those she has least use for see her best,*
> *Their paths grown craven and circuitous,*
> *Their visions mountain-clear, their needs immodest.*

Isn't it clear? It means that these people, these indigestible sterilities, see rebirth and resurrection most vividly and imaginatively, but it isn't for them; their way through life isn't a gay confident striding. What they *see* is clear and wonderful, but their needs are immodest in the sense that they want more girls and Jaguars than the normal amount other people get, because they get none.

Are you distinguishing yourself from that type of person?

No, that's me all right. Or was: you must remember it's all about thirty years ago.

Do you feel the poem 'Church Going' has been rather too much evaluated?

Over-valued, do you mean? Or analysed? I don't think I've seen much about it, except one chap who said it was too long. I think it all develops naturally enough. It came from the first time I saw a ruined church in Northern Ireland, and I'd never seen a ruined church before—discarded. It shocked me. Now of course it's commonplace: churches are not so much ruined as turned into bingo-halls, warehouses for refrigerators or split-level houses for architects.

It's not clear in the poem that you began with a ruined church.

No, it wasn't in the poem, but when you go into a church there's a feeling of something . . . well . . . over, derelict.

Some critics have discerned in it a yearning for a latter-day Christian or religious sanction. Is that so?

I suppose so. I'm not someone who's lost faith: I never had it. I was baptized—in Coventry Cathedral, oddly enough: the old one—but not confirmed. Aren't religions shaped in terms of what people want? No one could help hoping Christianity was true, or at least the happy ending—rising from the dead and our sins forgiven. One longs for these miracles, and so in a sense one longs for religion. But 'Church Going' isn't that kind of poem: it's a humanist poem, a celebration of the dignity of . . . well, you know what it says.

Could you comment on what one of your critics has said about The Less Deceived *as a whole: 'What saves [Larkin] from the limitations of the Movement is his occasional transcendence, without inappropriateness, of the commonplace.'?*

I never thought the Movement commonplace, if that's what's implied. Not like *Lyrical Ballads*. It was much wittier and more cerebral. I don't want to transcend the commonplace, I love the commonplace, I lead a very commonplace life. Everyday things are lovely to me.

If I can move on to The Whitsun Weddings, *which one of your less favourable critics has called 'a sad and even bitterly cynical book'* . . .

Eh? You can't say 'The Whitsun Weddings', which is central to the book, is a sad poem. It was just the transcription of a very happy afternoon. I didn't change a thing, it was just there to be written down.

Did you intend to give an unqualified assent to hopefulness at the end of the poem, where you seem to be flirting with a romantic visionary quality?

Yes. You couldn't be on that train without feeling the young lives all starting off, and that just for a moment you were touching them. Doncaster, Retford, Grantham, Newark, Peterborough, and at every station more wedding parties. It was wonderful, a marvellous afternoon. It only needed writing down. Anybody could have done it.

Elsewhere in your poems you've tended to moderate any hopefulness . . .

The Greeks used to spill a few drops of wine in propitiation of the Fates, didn't they. Perhaps it's like that. But it wasn't necessary in 'The Whitsun Weddings'. There's nothing to suggest that their lives won't be happy, surely? I defy you to find it.

Could one say the same about 'An Arundel Tomb'?

Well, that is rather a romantic poem; there's even less reservation in that. I don't like it much, partly because of this; technically it's a bit muddy in the middle—the fourth and fifth stanzas seem trudging somehow, with awful rhymes like voyage/damage. Everything went wrong with that poem: I got the hands wrong—it's right-hand gauntlet really—and anyway the hands were a nineteenth-century addition, not pre-Baroque at all. A friend of mine who visited the tomb in Chichester Cathedral told me that the guide said, 'A poem was written about this tomb by Philip Spender.' Muddle to the end.

But did you feel sceptical about the faithfulness that's preserved for us in stone?

No. I was very moved by it. Of course it was years ago. I think what survives of us is love, whether in the simple biological sense or just in terms of responding to life, making it happier, even if it's only making a joke. I was delighted when a friend asked me if I knew a poem ending 'What will survive of us is love.' It suggested the poem was making its way without me. I like them to do that.

I want to relate that to what you say about our sense of love in 'Faith Healing'—'across most it sweeps/As all they might have done had they been loved'—which does sound like a projection of one's own experience which might not match others' . . .

Well, people want to be loved, don't they. The sort of unconditional love parents give if you're lucky, and that gets mixed up with the love of God—'dear child', and so on. The poem came after seeing faith-healing in a film. 'At Grass' was a film too, about Brown Jack. You wouldn't remember him, a famous flat-racer and jumper, I think: there he was, completely forgotten and quite happy.

Is 'Naturally the Foundation will Bear Your Expenses' meant to be just a funny poem in which the speaker is the butt of the joke?

It's both funny and serious. The speaker's a shit. That's always serious.

It's seemed to some reviewers that you suffered from problems of identification with Mr Bleaney in 'Mr Bleaney', but it seems to me that perhaps they're missing the grammatical construction of the last two stanzas—'But if he . . . I don't know'—which both ventures a judgement and refuses it at the same time.

The first two-thirds of the poem, down to 'But if', are concerned with my uneasy feeling that I'm becoming Mr Bleaney, yes. The last third is reassuring myself that I'm not, because he was clearly quite content with his sauce instead of gravy, and digging the garden and so on, and yet there's doubt lingering too, perhaps he hated it as much as I did.

But to that extent you're not being presumptuous, judging him by what you sense yourself?

I don't think so. Unless you think it's presumptuous to judge anyone.

Do you think the poem has been given a false emphasis in your work?

Well, no, not a false one. Excessive, perhaps. I've never understood why it's so popular: I thought the subject was peculiar to me, and yet everybody seems to understand it and like it. When you're an only lodger, your relation with your landlady is very delicate: she's constantly urging you to do what she wants—dig the garden, or sit with her in the evenings, instead of sloping off to your own room.

The Whitsun Weddings *starts with the poem 'Here', which is sometimes read as a brief for retirement, the simpler life. Is that what you intended?*

Oh no, not at all . . . well, it all depends what you mean by retirement. If you mean not living in London, I suppose it might be interpreted along those lines. I meant it just as a celebration of here, Hull. It's a fascinating area, not quite like anywhere else. So busy, yet so lonely. The poem is frightful to read aloud: the first sentence goes on for twenty-four-and-a-half lines, which is three-quarters of the poem, and the rest is full of consonants.

I've read one article which speaks of a growing disenchantment in High Windows . . .

Just me getting older, I suppose. What's disenchanted about describing a hospital, or a nursing home?

I think the poem called 'High Windows' is slightly perplexing, since it starts on a vulgar level and shoots beyond it in the last stanza.

I think the end shows a desire to get away from it all, not unlike 'Dry-Point' in a way, or 'Absences'. I don't think it very good: I called the book after it because I liked the title. It's a true poem. One longs for infinity and absence, the beauty of somewhere you're not. It shows humanity as a series of oppressions, and one wants to be somewhere where there's neither oppressed nor oppressor, just freedom. It may not be very articulate.

Is it to be associated with the poem that stands before it in the book, 'Forget What Did', where you propose that a diary might be filled with 'observed/ Celestial recurrences'?

Yes, that's about getting away from the miseries of life as well. It's about a time when I stopped keeping a diary because I couldn't bear to record what was going on. I kept a diary for a long time, more as a kind of great grumble-book than anything else. It's stopped now.

Would you acknowledge that there's in fact more compassion and generosity in High Windows *as a whole . . .*

I should like to think so.

. . . as in poems like 'To the Sea', where you conclude with a sentiment about people 'helping the old, too, as they ought'?

My father died when my mother was sixty-one, and she lived to be ninety-one. We used to take a week's holiday in the summer. That poem came when we were in Southwold, when I realized that I hadn't had a 'seaside holiday' for years, and remembered all the ones when I was young.

It reminds me of what you wrote about William Barnes back in 1962—you rebuked him for being almost too gentle, too submissive and forgiving, and yet in a sense you seem to have arrived at that position yourself. You had reservations about the fact that Barnes didn't show Hardy's bitter and ironical despair.

He doesn't have Hardy's cutting edge, does he? The rhythms are so regular, and it's all a bit cosy. I'm glad if you do find the poems in *High Windows* more compassionate: I don't know that they are. But one must be more aware of suffering as one grows older, as we said earlier. I thought the poems were more of the same, you know. There are some quite nasty ones in it. 'They fuck you up, your mum and dad' doesn't sound very compassionate.

It's very funny, though.

It's perfectly serious as well.

In some poems you're taking the risk of sentiment brimming over into sentimentality.

Am I? I don't understand the word sentimentality. It reminds me of Dylan Thomas's definition of an alcoholic: 'A man you don't like who drinks as much as you do.' I think sentimentality is someone you don't like feeling as much as you do. But you can't win, can you?

Several of the poems can be docketed with your word 'beautiful', such as 'Cut Grass' or 'Solar' . . .

Yes, 'Solar' was the first poem I wrote after *The Whitsun Weddings*. Nobody's ever liked it, or mentioned it. It was unlike anything I'd written for about twenty years, more like *The North Ship*.

I suppose critics find it doesn't comport with the general run of what your poems say.

So much the worse for them. It's a feeling, not a thought. Beautiful.

Was it your intention, in using bad language in one or two poems, to provide a shock tactic?

Yes. I mean, these words are part of the palette. You use them when you want to shock. I don't think I've ever shocked for the sake of shocking. 'They fuck you up' is funny because it's ambiguous. Parents bring about your conception and also bugger you up once you are born. Professional parents in particular don't like that poem.

How did you come to write 'The Explosion', the last poem in the book?

I heard a song about a mine disaster; a ballad, a sort of folk song. I thought it very moving, and it produced the poem. It made me want to write the same thing, a mine disaster with a vision of immortality at the end—that's the point of the eggs. It may be all rather silly. I like it.

Looking back over all your work, what do you feel is the imaginative note that is peculiarly your own?

I don't know. You see, you don't write the poems you really want to write. I should like to write poems about how beautiful the world is and how wonderful people are, but the words somehow refuse to come. I don't think any of my poems are more typical of me than the rest. 'The Whitsun Weddings', 'The Explosion', 'Show Saturday', 'Coming', 'Absences'—no, I can't pick and choose. 'Send No Money' is the one I repeat to myself. Don't judge me by them. Some are better than me, but I add up to more than they do. One does one's best, and lets the result stand or fall by itself.

PAUL MULDOON

Were you brought up in a rural environment in Ulster?

Yes, I was, but not on a farm as such. I came to live in a place called Collegelands in north Armagh when I was about four, because my mother, who was a schoolteacher, got a job there. My father was essentially a labourer, and for some time a market gardener. He first grew cauliflowers and peas, and then moved to mushroom farming: that particular area of Armagh is an important mushroom-growing area, and there are also many orchards. But having said that, I should add that it's not essentially rural.

There's a nearby village called the Moy which figures quite strongly in my poems, though I've fictionalized it to a great extent. It's an area very rich in history and folklore, just as every square mile of Ireland is coming down with history and is burdened by it. The Moy itself was built by a man called James Caulfeild, who was at one stage Lord Lieutenant of Ireland, Earl of Charlemont, which is a little sister hamlet to the Moy. This story may be totally apocryphal, but Caulfeild is supposed to have designed it on the principle of an Italian town, Marengo. I've fictionalized the place to this extent—as I see it, one of my main duties as a writer is to write about what is immediately in front of me, or immediately over my shoulder. Clearly any landscape or locale is going to be re-mapped by a writer—Hardy's Wessex, Faulkner's Yoknapatawpha, Joyce's Dublin, Yeats Country—I'm not setting myself against any of them, but these are places which are recognizable in their fixtures yet are changed by the creative process. I'm very interested in the way in which a small place, a parish, can come to stand for the world. As I began to read I became aware that several writers—particularly those from the North like Seamus Heaney, Derek Mahon and Michael Longley—were writing about places I knew, and that what they had to say about them was accepted beyond those places.

You were brought up with a religion?

Yes, I was brought up as a Catholic. Both my parents were Catholic. My poem called 'The Mixed Marriage' is not about a marriage mixed by religion. I merely try to some extent to describe them and their relationship. They would have been something like the Morels—though that's an overstated comparison—in *Sons and Lovers*. My father is anything but a coarse, lumbering man—he's a very refined man—but not educated. My mother was the youngest of a large family, and she was the only one they could afford to educate, so she went to a teacher's training college in Belfast.

The poem seems to present the sort of geometry which might have led to a division in yourself.

Yes, and being geometrical its edges are rather sharp. The Latin Quarter, Proust, and Castor and Pollux is perhaps over-simply set against the hole in the hedge, the life lived close to the earth.

Do you feel that you've shown more loyalty to your mother's career in following a life in letters, while at the same time harking back to the rurality of your father?

To begin with, I don't see myself as a man of letters. But I suppose that in the second book, *Mules*, I was trying to explore these lives that couldn't quite reproduce themselves, and that were sterile in themselves. It's too programmatic to describe it in these terms . . . but lives caught between heaven and earth. The poem 'Mules' itself: the mule is the offspring of a jack-ass and a mare, and the mare came to stand for me as some sort of basic earth force—a pagan force, if we can use that word—an animal that was worshipped by the Celts. On the other hand, the donkey is significant in Christian mythology.

Through living in Ireland and having the kind of education I had, I was very much aware of the Irish language and history, and of the energy of the Celtic civilization. When I went to grammar school, St. Patrick's College in Armagh, I came under quite exceptional influences. One man, Sean O'Boyle, who was a scholar of the Irish language and music, taught me Irish and gave me, and everyone round me, a sense of this marvellous heritage of literature and song in Gaelic. I was also blessed—it may sound corny, but I really do feel blessed—by a man called Gerry Hicks, a singer, who taught English. They were people whose knowledge exuded from them. A man called John McCarter really started me writing, I suppose. He'd been involved, peripherally I think, in the Dublin literary scene, and he gave me the sense that there were writers alive in Dublin. He also introduced me to the *Faber Book of Modern Verse*, which I more or less learned off by heart. He introduced me to T. S. Eliot, whom I thought was God, though I no longer think that. When he set English essays for the weekend, I wrote a poem, which seemed a much shorter and simpler thing to do. I'm a great believer in that definition of poetry as the stuff that doesn't quite reach the margins. I got away with it again and again, with the upshot that I didn't do very well in English Language exams. That's how I got started.

Was your experience at Queen's University, Belfast, equally fulfilling?

I met Seamus Heaney and Michael Longley just before I left grammar school in 1968, and I asked Seamus if he'd look at my poems if I sent them to him. He subsequently published a couple of them in a magazine he was then editing. Strangely enough the very first poems I had published were in Irish, but I soon gave that up because, though I'd studied Irish, I didn't have a real control of the language. Heaney was my tutor at Queen's, and there was a lot happening at Belfast—the aftermath of the famous London group that Philip Hobsbaum had run when he taught at Belfast. Hobsbaum had left, but the group was still in operation—Heaney, Longley, various other writers, and a very good critic called Michael Allen who teaches at Queen's. There were weekly meetings, for a time in Seamus Heaney's house, and later in a pub, where new poems were discussed. It was very important for me, since a writer must be a good critic of his work. There was no sloppiness in the group, everyone was quite outspoken. It was a very healthy kind of society, and I use the word 'society' to describe the group. It's scarcely a group at all, even though it's become a critical convenience to see them as presenting a united front to the world: you have only to read them to be aware of the variety. They're not united by any kind of manifesto.

Do you feel you're answerable as much to the principles of that group as to your own imaginative direction?

I think one can only be faithful to the language and the way in which it presents itself to you, and to the world in the way it presents itself to you . . . faithful in the sense of the meeting between language and experience. I believe in inspiration, it's a valid way of describing the process of being open. My poems begin with a couple of ideas which try to work themselves out into some kind of shape.

A number of your poems seem to work a single image . . .

I'm very interested in the Metaphysicals and in the conceit. I look on each poem as being a little world in itself. I'm very interested in the narrative, the story, and in wanting almost to write novels in the poem. I like to think that a whole society is informing the lines of a poem, that every detail is accurate. And I'm interested in the dramatic persona. I like using different characters, to present different views of the world.

I think the writer who excited me most at university was Robert Frost: an apparently simple, almost naïve, tone of voice and use of language, underneath which all kinds of complex things are happening. I believe very firmly that the most complex notions in the world can be presented in a simple, immediate way, and can have a primary, direct effect on the reader. If you take a poem like Frost's 'The Road Not Taken', the complexity is astounding, and yet it just flies off the page.

What you're saying immediately makes me think of your poem 'The Country Club' . . .

Yes, the first eight lines of that poem are taken directly from Frost's 'The Mountain'. It's a strange poem. I was trying, I suppose, to write about being implicated in a society, and more specifically in a violent event in a society—implicated simply by being on the sidelines. In my first book, a poem called 'Party Piece' concerns characters who wished for 'the explosion's heart'—where in fact you're least likely to get damaged, I'm told—'not/Pain's edge where we take shelter'. In 'The Field Hospital', the characters, for all their rather blasé view of blood and gore, are on the edge but implicated. That poem partly emerged from a viewing of the film *M.A.S.H.*, and a viewing of *The Good, The Bad and The Ugly*, the spaghetti Western in which, I would guess, the Civil War scenes must be a most faithful reconstruction of what it would have been like; also the fact that when I was sitting in the house in Ardboe one night a big yellow moth came in the window and landed on my sleeve.

Do you regard Frost as a model in your work, or do you have many models?

I don't think there are any models as such. I don't care very much for the notion of a single canon of a poet's work to which one must be faithful. I like a great number of poems by a great number of people from Michael Drayton to Craig Raine. Frost was important to me early on because his line, his tone of voice, was so much a bare canvas. He's a good man to learn from in that he has no particular nervous tics, no characteristics but the strong, classic, lyric line. But the most important thing for me in Frost was his mischievous, sly, multi-layered quality under the surface. One thing that does come across for me in my own poems is a wryness, a mischievousness in the voice, and I'm never quite sure whether I want to believe that voice, this person who's presenting a piece of the world to me.

The wryness you speak of is not something which you first intended but something you now recognize in your voice after three books?

Indeed, I think it's unfortunate and dangerous that I can recognize it. One is running very grave risks of self-parody in becoming overly self-conscious, self-aware. I think by and large I've escaped that, since I'm interested in ventriloquism, in speaking through other people, other voices. I suppose some kind of tone creeps through but I don't want to locate it: I'm not pleading for ignorance but against circumspection. The writer's duty is to be open, and not to have too many preconceptions about how it is and how it should be set down.

Do you acknowledge my feeling that in a number of poems you're trying to catechize certain received attitudes of the Irish, mythical and legendary . . . St. Brendan and his boat, for example? Are you conscious of refusing to take history and tradition on trust?

Yes, and this goes back to what we were saying about the voice: we mustn't take anything at face value, not even the man who is presenting things at face value. For all our simplifications of the world—and a work of art is a simplification in terms of its process of selection, a continual reduction of the variables in what a thing might mean—that process of simplification must not become simplistic. We all know that if we try to nail a thing down it can pull the nail out and walk away, and perhaps that has something to do with my slyness and wryness. The poem can engage for thirty seconds in a little fiction: it has moved me, it will hopefully move you, disturb you, excite you; and having said and done that, we go our separate ways back into the welter.

Would you say that you detect a strong moral drive in your work?

It's apparent to me as a reader of the poems in *New Weather* in particular, many of which I don't like because of exactly that tone. I don't happen to like the moralizing tone in myself. Of course, you may not like how you are, but you have to accept that that's how it is, or was. So many of the last lines in *New Weather* come thumping off the soap-box, like 'None could describe/ Electrocution, falling, the age of innocence'—how more ponderous can you get? . . . or 'Yet by my broken bones/I tell new weather'—which is silly and imperious.

It's a kind of knowing tone you indulged as a younger man, but not all the poems are of that kind.

No, 'The Cure for Warts' seems all right, though it uses a slightly tricksy typographical switch from 'nippling' to 'nibbling'. Well, it's apparently tricksy, but to describe those warts as 'nippling' and 'nibbling' is reasonably accurate: I can tell you that because they're my own warts which I transposed to someone else. I'm very much against revision, however, since those poems were written at a particular time. I view the business of writing as a way of dealing with how we are. We keep changing, but we can't deny how we were at that given moment.

Do you have a sense of coordination between one poem and another in Why Brownlee Left *or in* Mules, *of certain consistent imaginative notes being struck, and of an order to each book?*

I think both those books do run the risk of *appearing* slightly programmatic in that, in each case, only two or three concerns recur. They just happen to be ideas which obsessed me for two or three years, and still do. In *Why Brownlee Left* I'm interested in random behaviour, in swervings, deviations: and set against that a sense of purpose and idealism, be it in terms of romantic views of women or ideal societies or revolutionary politics. The sort of thing Buñuel explored in *That Obscure Object of Desire*.

So you have a sense of unity about that book as perhaps never before? It builds through each poem.

Yes, I think it does. I think a poem should be intact in itself, but I think interesting things happen when a number of poems come out of a single, if dislocated, personality. They're bound to have some kind of unity. I've become very interested in structures that can be fixed like mirrors at angles to each other—it relates to narrative form—so that new images can emerge from the setting up of the poems in relation to each other: further ironies are possible, further mischief is possible. I hope the mischief I make is of a rewarding kind, not that of a practical joker, and will outline the complexities of being here.

The resonances of a poem like 'Anseo' seem immense in that respect ... since it treats the possibilities of behaviouristic conditioning in a rather chilling way.

If it works, it works because everything in it is absolutely dead-on, the details in it are really accurate. It's fiction, of course.

I suppose one must make a distinction between the poet using his words as a register of experience and using them as an interpretation of that experience, perhaps making quite a purposeful comment on a situation, though not necessarily in a ratiocinative or diagnostic way?

Yes, a poem does make a comment; if you live in a society, you're bound to reflect what happens in that society. That becomes complicated in the case of living in the North of Ireland. The poems I've written about the political situation there tend to be oblique, and I think properly so: they tend to look slightly farther back at the society from which the situation erupted, at *why* we are how we are now. What can you say about *how* we are? What I have to say about the politics of Northern Ireland is no more significant, probably much less informed, than what A, B or C has to say; it's pure opinion. Of course there is a place in poetry for opinion, but there's no place for the opinionated. If I believed there were a revolution, for example, and you can take it that I *don't*—I don't believe that Catholics are good guys and Protestants are bad guys, or vice-versa—if we were living in a banana republic and were being truly, monstrously oppressed, one can imagine pamphleteering, but not in Northern Ireland. The society is much too complex. 'Anseo' is about a very complex society indeed.

Do you think that at the least the attitude should be valid within the terms of the form and language of the poem?

Clearly one's allegiances, or bigotries, are going to be hinted at or guessed at, though I have no proper allegiances except to tell it like it is.

If you're saying that we have to make imaginative discriminations, I think you're quite right, but would you say that as a poet living in Ulster you have to strive for an immunity from political and historical pressures, or has it become necessary for you to assimilate them and try to synthesize them? Does the oppressive quality of life put an undue pressure on your writing? I mean, obliquity can pretend to be a poetic in its own right.

Sure, and I might appear to be evasive. But I don't have committed beliefs—it's as simple as that. Perhaps one makes a virtue of the necessity of how one is. I consider it important that I shouldn't have preconceptions, or that if I have them they shouldn't get in the way of the language, which I suppose is what I'm really interested in. I'm in awe of the language. But I'm not just in love with words, they've got to take on shapes that mean something. I think my response is quite responsible. In 'Early Warning', the figure of 'Our Protestant neighbour, Billy

Wetherall' is not aware of his mess. I myself grew up, through geography lessons, to think of Northern Ireland as a linen-weaving, ship-building Utopia, and there's just no denying that when the Protestants had power they misused it. The poem is saying all that, but in no way as directly as I'm saying it now. Which would you prefer? All the things that are happening in the poem are true of a Catholic response, if you want to read it most overtly in that way: it's using all the clichés about Catholics and Protestants—Catholics have loads of children, they are notoriously given to factions, and they depend on more than they can see in terms of their religion and in terms of their Nationalist aspirations . . .

. . . and all that is conveyed by the images, not by exposition.

Right. What I object to is that to précis what's happening in the poem the way I'm doing now is to overstate it, to make it crude, and not to allow for the complexity of the poem. The poems are true and they make statements, but they're not standing on a box at Speaker's Corner. 'Anseo' is a very strong statement, if you want to read the poem that way: it's saying the society from which the child emerges is an oppressive, cruel one, and it's a Catholic society. I'm saying it now, but it's more powerfully embodied in the poem.

And another factor is that the figure of Joseph Mary Plunkett Ward makes a virtue of being oppressed.

Yes. I know these people, and some of them love the notion of being oppressed. The society that Joe Ward posits for the future, the society that the IRA posits for the future, is not a society I want to know. I'm making these crude statements now only to underline how much more *effectively* I do it in verse. 'Lunch with Pancho Villa' (*Mules*) is a poem in which the old pamphleteer is upbraiding the protagonist in the kind of way that I might be upbraided—

> 'Look, son. Just look around you.
> People are getting themselves killed
> Left, right and centre
> While you do what? Write rondeaux?

There's more to living in this country
Than stars and horses, pigs and trees,
Not that you'd guess it from your poems.
Do you never listen to the news?
You want to get down to something true,
Something a little nearer home.'

—and my point is that an understanding of the people who keep those pigs and shelter under those trees is true, and *is* at home.

I'd like to ask you here about your long poem 'Immram' in Why Brownlee Left . . .

Yes . . . 'Immram' means 'voyage tale'. Under the influence of the *Navigatio Sancti Brendani* the earlier forms of voyage tales were given a Christian veneer. One of the best known of them is 'Immram Mael Duin' (another is the 'Voyage of Bran', which partly explains a small joke in an earlier poem), in which the hero sets out to avenge his father's death, goes through many fabulous adventures, and at the end discovers an old hermit sitting on a rock—who turns out to be a Howard Hughes figure in my version—who tells him that he should turn the other cheek. Swift was very likely aware of the genre, and Tennyson has a dreadful version of it. I've tried to write a version which gives it a contemporary setting, because one of the few genres in which the heroic mode is possible is the thriller. Apart from that, I like Chandler a great deal; I think he's a very good writer, a good stylist. Byron is knocking around there too.

Are you faithful to the individual episodes of 'Immram Mael Duin'?

My poem takes the episodes and motifs of the original and twists them around, sometimes out of all recognition. At one stage, for instance, a confrontation with a white cat becomes a confrontation with a black cat . . .

. . . which is slang for a black.

Yes.

'Immram' runs a real risk of appearing a piece of sheer ventriloquism, but it does pull together a lot of the things that the book concerns itself with: the central notion, for example, of the Howard Hughes figure who lives at the top of an hotel with a deserted floor just underneath him . . . that whole sense of the layers of perception is something I try to explore in other poems. One of the things that set me off was this vision of an old hermit who's visited every day by an otter bringing him a loaf of bread and a jug of ale, which I treat in terms of Hughes's penchant for Baskin-Robbins banana-nut ice-cream. The quest is the powerful and important centre of the poem. Both the protagonist and his father are led through a maze. The protagonist is a cipher, the world envelops him, everything happens to him; he directs very little, and I'm very sceptical about how much we direct anything that happens to us. And the end of it is this whimsical—I would tend to use the word 'whimful', which doesn't exist—this whimsical dismissal by the bane of both their lives. 'I forgive you . . . and I forget'.

How does the earlier, shorter poem 'Immrama' relate to 'Immram'?

I wrote it some time ago, when I had no notion of writing the longer poem, though certainly with a sense of 'Immram Mael Duin' at the back of my head. In a way, 'Immrama' is a poem about never having been born . . . the father leads a totally different life (which he might easily have done) in which I would not have figured. 'Immrama' means 'voyages'; it's the plural of 'Immram'.

As you say, it's consistent with certain motifs in the book as a whole: the possibility of alternative lives, capricious disappearances, the possibility that certain figures might have been the victims of sectarian killings or might just have opted out.

Yes . . . as to why Brownlee left, for example. That poem began, I think, when I saw a photograph of two horses standing in a field, or perhaps I *did* see two horses—such a powerful image—and I started to think about what might have happened. The name itself, Brownlee, suggests a brown meadow, a ploughed field, and so—in a strange sort of way—his end is in his name; he's fulfilled his purpose even before he begins. I use names perhaps far too often in a Jonsonian, emblematic way.

Why do you think the notion of alternative lives is peculiarly fetching, philosophically attractive, to your imagination?

I think it's central to us. One of the ways in which we are most ourselves is that we imagine ourselves to be going somewhere else. It's important to most societies to have the notion of something out there to which we belong, that our home is somewhere else ... there's another dimension, something around us and beyond us, which is our inheritance. There are undesirable elements to that wish to be elsewhere, in the form, for instance, of escapism.

Would you say that you're looking for an imagined order, though the phrase has religious overtones?

It's pretty well established in my mind that the world has an order. There is an order among things which has got to do with more than our ordering of them, our perception of them.

Several of the poems in Why Brownlee Left *have more comedy than you've managed in earlier books.*

A lot of them should be read as rather funny. The tone of voice, the slightly tongue-in-cheek quality, allows for humour and irony.

Can you say why you've been drawn, on the whole, to work in forms of established prosody, stanzaic patterns, and rhyme?

Sometimes, I'm sure, there's an element of laziness about it. The only use I can see for formal structures is to help the writer himself decide the shape and size of the canvas. What has to be said determines its own form, or should do. It then helps the reader to have some kind of fixity. I don't scan, however, but use a purely intuitive process within each line. My only concern is that the lines are speakable. I have rather loose notions of what a rhyme is, since many of mine are assonantal. I've been described as someone who would rhyme 'cat' with 'dog'. But I've also managed 'moon' and 'June'.

D. E. S. Maxwell, in an essay which took brief stock of your early work, said that your world is threatening, and at times disheartening. Is that an aspect of your work that you recognize or that has gone further?

Disheartening? I find it difficult to talk about, since it goes back to a 'view of the world'. I would say it's not disheartening. But it's not always a barrel of laughs, is it?

Anything that swims into your world picture is *in* your world picture. That's why I'm very much against expressing a categorical view of the world. I hope I can continue to discover something, and not to underline or bolster up what I already think I know.

RICHARD MURPHY

Can I ask you a biographical question to begin with: do you regret the schooling you had, which took you away from Ireland? Did it accentuate a dilemma you may have felt in yourself, being partly Irish and partly English, or did it help in the long run to put your values into perspective?
I never stayed longer than two years in any one school: the first near Dublin, the second (perhaps a little longer than two years) at Canterbury leading up to the time of Dunkirk. In locating myself in the west of Ireland, I've had to make myself belong here. Now I'm leaving the west, but it will always be the landscape of my imagination. I've found a site in Dublin which makes it possible for me to say that I'm moving from granite to granite. Fourteen years ago I built my house here out of stone I took from some derelict cottages. I'm moving to a house in the middle of a garden of granite outcrop. I think I've always looked for that kind of security—a place to which I belong, a house which is well built—because of the insecurity of my life and parts of my upbringing: an insecurity brought on by the war, and by my own loss of faith in Christianity, and by the fall of the British Empire in whose strength I was reared. For a long time I felt disturbed by being regarded as an Englishman because of my British accent, and yet feeling more self-consciously Irish in England than I ever would at home.
Your father was in Colonial Service, so presumably you didn't see much of him?
He spent thirty years of his life in Ceylon and I spent some of my very early years there too; I can remember it from the age of four to seven. The five poems about Ceylon in *High Island* are all

about a time when I was six years old. My memories of it are rather frightening: fear of poison, disease, malaria, scorpions and snakes. I was absolutely terrified of being stung by a mosquito and dying of malaria. My mother got the MBE for establishing hospitals during a malaria epidemic. My fear of poison was very much associated with a sense of guilt, and the sense of guilt was part of the culture, of imperialism. A sense of guilt on the one hand coupled with a tremendous sense of assurance on the other—that it was extremely fortunate that God had agreed that we should be born speaking English, that all other languages would have to be translated into English to make sense; God, after all, was prayed to in English. Anybody who wasn't born speaking this language seemed to me to be at a great disadvantage.

Is that the reason why you interwove the Ceylon poems with Irish poems in High Island, *by way of establishing a parallelism between one culture and another?*

Why I mixed them up and didn't keep them as a group? Well, I should acknowledge that the arrangement of the poems in *High Island* was done with the advice and help and under the scrutiny of my friend Tony White. He regarded it really as a matter of arranging a vase of flowers—you mix them up, but mix them up in a way that the themes recur. A certain number are juxtaposed, facing each other; for example, 'The Glass Dump Road' is followed by 'High Island', the lowest is followed by the highest note in the book.

But each poem had its own occasion?

Yes. In 'Nocturne' facing 'Sunup', for instance, there's a certain reason for the juxtaposition in that I associate in the back of my mind the storm petrel with the tinker, the traveller.

If I can pick you up on the sense of guilt you've spoken of, which normally goes with a corresponding sense of responsibility: where does your responsibility lie? Perhaps you can say how you reconcile your care for tinker families with a life of the imagination, books and art? Do you feel that the aspects of your life fit together?

The trouble is, they strain against each other. My close connection with travellers began really after I'd built my house here. It was partly feeling that I was extremely fortunate to live in such a marvellously well-built house with pink granite walls and green quarry slates from Westmorland, and then discovering that some of the tinker families lived all their lives under canvas and wattle tents on the road behind the bank and the forge leading down to the dump in inland towns. I tried to find out how this came about.

Has your role been an avuncular or paternalistic one? Did they at first regard you as the lord of the manor arriving to distribute largesse?

This is an afterthought, but I can best express it in terms of a poem I haven't actually written yet . . . as you drive through the country you quite often pass the ruins of an old demesne wall, probably built by labour before and during the Famine at fourpence or sixpence a day, in order to give employment to the starving tenantry, and also to enhance the prestige of the local landlord (if he could surround his 500-acre estate with a big high wall he was a match for his neighbours); and it helped to keep out poachers and tinkers who frequently camped up against the demesne wall because it gave shelter. My first meeting with tinkers was when they'd come to my grandparents' house to beg or to steal hens or to mend cans and kettles. I was always rather frightened of them because of their reputation for stealing and for being verminous, and for being thoroughly brutal to their horses and donkeys, which were covered in sores, and also brutal to their wives and children: the epitome of all that was worst in Ireland. You notice now that these derelict demesnes are frequently favourite places for tinkers to camp; the council will often give them caravans and they'll camp around what used to be the gate lodge. There is and always has been a certain affinity between, as Yeats has it, the noble and the beggarman. In a sense, some people would say, neither really belonged to the country, they were both outsiders of completely different kinds.

It was after I gave up being a fisherman in Cleggan that I made friends with a family who were itinerant, and as a fisherman I had belonged much more to the village than I have done in the last ten years. I built my house in Cleggan because I had a boat which was tied up at the quay, and the boat had the function of sailing with people to Inishbofin during the summer, taking them fishing. I had the *Ave Maria* and the *Truelight*, a sister ship, and they provided jobs for three men in the village as well as myself. I lived on that business, which was a great struggle to run and scarcely profitable, for about seven years, from 1960 to 1967. I took to the sea because I wanted to write about the sea, and I found that a lot of sea poetry struck me as being rather too metaphorical in the 1950s. I didn't think that I could write well about the sea until I had some practical experience of being at sea. I wanted to tell the story of the Cleggan Disaster as truly as I could to the experience of the fishermen of the coast to whom it happened, and I felt the best way to do it was to live that life myself for a while.

Do you feel most drawn to descriptive and narrative poetry, then?

Yes, at that time. What I really wanted to do was to simplify my life and to find a kind of bedrock on which I could build, and to get to know the heart of the country in which I'd been born, which was totally different to the world in which I'd been brought up, Ceylon and England. It was a kind of exploration, my coming to Connemara, becoming a fisherman, buying the *Ave Maria* and doing her up and writing a poem celebrating her life, and then writing a poem celebrating the courage and endurance of one fisherman in the storm. That poem, 'The Cleggan Disaster', was really, I suppose, about my own effort to survive the break-up of my marriage and the feeling of futility which came over me after it, but that is hindsight. The poem is about a man who survived by not giving up and by facing the storm, using his skill and his knowledge of the currents under the water to counteract the storm in the air, as opposed to the boys in the boat who tell him to give up and say prayers and let the boat drift. I admired that stance, and I tried to imitate it in my own seamanship. Building the house was a confirmation of that process and of the belief that we were not going to be done down by the storm which happened in 1927—the year I was born—and by the whole disaster mood of the country.

Up to the 1960s this country was beladen with that sense that art isn't worth your while; it's been tried before and failed, you won't catch any fish or you'll get wrecked in a storm. Why bother going out, there are easier ways to live? In Dublin some of my predecessors impressed me poorly by the self-destructive nature of their lives, drinking themselves to death. This village, Cleggan, was synonymous with disaster, and nobody had gone out fishing since 1927; it looked as if it had been bombed. For two years I was the only person in the village who owned a boat that fished from the quay—and now there are lots of boats and I don't have a boat at all, I never go fishing. It both helped and interfered with my writing. It was an alternative to writing reviews for the *TLS* or the *Spectator*, a renouncing of the literary life. I felt it was purer, there was something purifying about the action. In cities I just got into a state of confusion and nervousness and a loss of identity other than that of somebody who was rather ambitious, which I didn't like. There was a loss in that renunciation as well, because it was a limiting of vocabulary.

I had been making this kind of move away from cities far out into the west of Ireland much of my life; it started when I was nineteen at Oxford by going down in mid-term. I did go back and finish my degree afterwards, but what I wanted to do then was to live in a cottage by a waterfall with a little oak wood at the head of a lake, and to write a blank verse play about a Mayor of Galway who had hanged his son some time in the Middle Ages. Later, by living in the west, I wanted to get down to my own roots, to simplify my life and master a simpler vocabulary. In writing 'The Cleggan Disaster' I set myself the task of using no word that wasn't current among the local fishermen. When I read it first to Pat Concannon, on whose life story it was based, he was quiet for a little after I'd finished, and then he said, 'What you've said is true, and it's well put together.' That was the praise I most wanted to hear.

Can you explain further how you associate the act of simplifying your personal life with writing the kind of poem you desired?

In 1963 Graham Martin said that there was nothing Irish about me except that I happened to write about Irish places; but in going down to the bedrock in the language I went down to Anglo-Saxon, which I'm glad to have studied at Oxford, and that's what came through. In fact, when I was writing 'The Last Galway Hooker', I derived the rhythm of the poem to some extent from *Sir Gawain and The Green Knight* as well as directly from the sea, the rhythm of the waves. It was really alliteration breaking as an undercurrent through the iambic blank verse measure—that's what I got through to, I think.

My father was reared in Clifden, seven miles from here—my grandfather was rector of Clifden—and my grandmother on my mother's side came from a place twenty miles from Cleggan, so that it was really home ground but it was nevertheless a home that I had to invent, to make for myself. I wanted to write with clarity, something that Philip Larkin had perfectly managed in his library. Beautiful lucidity! I admire his work enormously.

But do you not feel that your self-consciousness about your style of life and the subjects you wanted to explore may have inhibited the process of your poetry?

I'm trying to be aware now, but at the time it was instinct and intuition that drew me here, and also repulsion. I'd been repelled by city life, and repelled by myself in a city. I now feel nervous and trepid about moving back to a city.

During the early 1950s, when you were writing reviews, one of the things you seemed to look for in poetry was discipline and statement, a mastery of language, which might be held in opposition to someone like Seamus Heaney who addresses himself to the task in terms of surrender, of being a suppliant to the language. Do you in fact affirm a sense of dominance towards the language, a masculine rather than a feminine posture?

Heaney does also regard Ireland as being under the tutelage of the goddess, and England under the male god militant, and I think he's got something there. I think my English education had a strong military bias, and my mother's ancestors were in the British army, generations of colonels, generals, captains, majors. I tried to work this out in *The Battle of Aughrim*, to see my own conflict in historical terms.

But speaking more generally, has your own formalism in poetry provided a sufficient reward for you, the idea that you should conquer and govern words rather than allow yourself access to what the language gives you? You seem to have aimed at disciplining words.

Is that something you've detected in my poetry?

To some extent, yes, but more in your yesteryear reviews.

It's something I wouldn't be proud of now. Let's put it this way, there are two poems in *High Island* about the same bird, one is 'Song for a Corncrake' and the other 'Corncrake', and they face each other. Now 'Song for a Corncrake' is rhymed and lyrical, and it took me three weeks of hard work and discipline to write, wrestling; and 'Corncrake' took me thirty minutes, and it's in free verse. I don't think there's any advantage in having worked for three weeks, except if there was no sign of having worked at the end of it all—that the art would in the end appear quite artless. I hope it doesn't show there that I worked hard. I think some of the pieces in *The Battle of Aughrim* do show that they were nailed and hammered together, forged with labour and sweat. It's been necessary for me to work hard at my art, but I think it's a weakness in the art if it shows. A recent poem, for example, 'Shelter', which is in *Selected Poems*, I wrote straight out, a loosely-formed sonnet. Such a poem is a gift, and it's wonderful to receive those gifts, but I've only received those gifts at times when I've also been working at other things. They don't come through idleness.

You have set yourself some extremely difficult metrical and prosodic exercises, if I can say that without meaning to be pejorative. Is it fair for me to infer that you undertake certain poems in a spirit of some detachment from the subject matter?

I think that the form now comes up through the language itself. One of the reasons why I write is to try to keep certain people alive in words, and before I stopped in March I was writing poems about Tony White, who died over three years ago. I'd written nothing about him for the first couple of years after he died, though I'd thought about him continually, felt his loss every day and still do; but then I started to write the first of several poems about him, and it came out in very strict rhymes—effortlessly, which is unusual for me since I find rhyming rather difficult. I thought as I wrote that the rhymes were coming almost too easily, but that poem was written out of necessity and I think that's how poetry should be written—out of need. It came from the depths and was part of the person it was about. Subsequently I've written two or three more poems about him, and they've taken longer to write but they've all been equally intricate in form, partly because, although he seemed to his friends to be the freest person they knew, his freedom depended on a concealed self-discipline. He's the person to whom Thom Gunn's poem 'Innocence' is dedicated, a poem which also has a very strong form; Gunn's form manages to hold and to distance this terrible subject matter, to cool the fire sufficiently so that it becomes bearable and not just shocking or disgusting.

Why do you extol the act of distancing?

I think I may have a fear of passion being too strong and overwhelming, and it's certainly part of the English culture, not making a fuss about an accident or disaster.

Is that something you now regret?

I would love to be able to feel like Akhmatova in her beautiful reminiscences of Modigliani in Paris in 1910 and 1911—the purity, the passion, in her prose. But I'm not Russian.

I think that Edna Longley, writing about The Battle of Aughrim, *has remarked about a certain 'exteriority'.*[1] *I can see what she meant, although I don't feel it was any limitation in a poem which has so many formal strengths, since your qualities of discipline and masculinity seemed absolutely right for that sort of utterance. Presumably you were trying there to control the complex forces at work, and even the antinomies in your own heritage?*

I was trying, I think, to draw up a very complicated equation of the divisive forces in Irish history, and in myself, and in everybody in Ireland. At the centre of the equation was this great historical event, which resulted in the Protestant Ascendancy for the next two hundred years. That is true history, and out of this many myths had been made, causing further bloodshed. I felt that the final solution to the problem was to cool it by trying to understand what really happened and why. I hope I made it clear that nobody gained except a few landlords.

[1] 'Searching the Darkness: the Poetry of Richard Murphy, Thomas Kinsella, John Montagne and James Simmons', Douglas Dunn (ed.), *Two Decades of Irish Writing*, Carcanet Press, Cheadle Hulme, 1975.

The poem is about a colonial war, and it was an analogue of the Vietnam War. I felt at the time that poetry about Vietnam was far too raw and crude and immediate, too instant, and that a better way of dealing with war would be to look at it at a distance. Here you had the two major world powers, the Protestant nations allied to William of Orange, contending against the Catholic Louis Quatorze, and conducting their battles on the soil of a weak foreign dependent country whose natives were starving, and Louis sent the Marquis of St. Ruth as Commander-in-Chief to Ireland, because his wife complained to the king that he was cruel to her. The battle was really fought because of the vanity of St. Ruth. The Irish Catholic army was commanded by a French general who didn't speak Irish, the English army was commanded by a Dutchman: rather an ironic situation. I felt that some of the myths which inspired our loyalties were nonsense, and should be rejected. So it's in parts an anti-mythological poem. I hope that it's an historical poem, and I think there is poetry in history. Coolness was necessary, I felt, in dealing with a subject so hot. I tried to work out all the myths involved in the battle, the beliefs that made people fight. The poetry is a kind of geometry of the forces on both sides, and of the tragic consequences—the Flight of the Wild Geese, the Penal Laws, etc. The myths that inspire the IRA and the Orange Lodges were forged on that battlefield, some of them no doubt based on false reports and errors of judgement. At a moment when the Irish were winning, a cannonball shot off the head of the Marquis of St. Ruth, who hadn't divulged his tactics to the Irish generals for fear of treachery. I say in the poem, 'Chance, skill and treachery all hit the mark.' The condition of Irish politics today is still governed by that shot. The poem is personal in that my ancestors were involved on both sides, Catholic as well as Protestant. My feelings, I think, were more towards the Catholic suffering side; more critical of my conquering Protestant forbears.

Do you still deplore the Irish attachment to a sentimental view of history?

If you take the example of the Casement poem from *The Battle of Aughrim:* when Casement landed in Ireland from a German submarine, there was only a policeman to welcome him, and the policeman arrested him, but when Casement's calcified bones were flown back to Ireland after being dug up from a British gaol, there was a guard of honour and a state funeral. That struck me as indicating something very wrong with our society, this excessive adulation of the calcified bones of a person who got absolutely no support whatever from the people while he was alive. The irony of that appals me, and I deplore the cult of funerals in Ireland.

You seem to have decried personal expressiveness over the years.

I think I was probably expecting something more, either to replace the lost religion or something on a par with a symbolic order. I reject that now; I believe now in a more personal poetry, the celebration of an individual life, the personal life.

Is that the sort of poetry you're writing more and more?

Yes, poems like those about Tony White, and the short lyric about Mary Ure in *Selected Poems*.

Are they still in strict forms?

Yes, but not for any doctrinaire reason. The subject seemed to require the form. (In *High Island* I've several poems in free verse—they might not seem very free to habitual readers of the *American Poetry Review*, but they are free for me—such as 'Double Negative'.) My latest poem, 'A Bookcase for the OED', is in two stanzas of six lines each, every line ending with the letter 'd' but changing the vowel sounds. The verse form is a kind of coffin, like the binding of a book. But the form only emerged in the course of writing what I wanted to say.

Which poets do you feel you've drawn most sustenance from? In some ways, perhaps, from Robert Frost, for his narrative power?

Well, Yeats continually, and Hardy; Larkin and Hughes. Hughes's poetry is very different from mine, wonderfully fertile and explosive, hot, passionate.

At some stage in your prose writing I think you regretted the whole movement of modernity—what we now think of as Modernism—and preferred to set store by a sense of the continuity of English verse. You pointed out, for example, that Pound was a greater lyricist than Swinburne, the burden of your argument being that modernism seems like an accident, what I think you called a 'gesture' or novelty, and that what we should stress is the continuousness of verse traditions. Is that a view you still hold?

Yes, in that sense I'm a traditionalist. I don't think forms are either alive or dead, I think forms are the nature of things, things as they are, that we have to accept. In using them we make them live, or else they die in our hands. The classicist, if you like to use that word, tends to accept things as they are and find freedom in the acceptance of limits. The romantic, on the other hand, the idealist, tries to discard the limits, to extend them, to get rid of them, to pretend they're not there, to die in the process and be adored for it. The classicist is more of a realist. I think my attachment to form in language is connected with my love of music—English church music and psalms which I used to sing as a chorister in Canterbury Cathedral. My love of the architecture of Canterbury Cathedral is very deep, and it carries on in my love of the oratories and cells of the hermits of the seventh century on these islands off the western coast of Ireland, which I've tried to echo in my building of this house. I do see poems as buildings and as music, there's a strong element of architecture in my poetry. The dictionary—this is really crucial—belongs to the world of dead literature, and so do bookshelves, and yet they contain the seed that a person can sow, the seed of living speech, the seed that can always be revived, as our friends cannot be revived.

Do you feel sanguine about the state of poetry now, and that important poems are being written?

I do, yes, and by people younger than myself, particularly Seamus Heaney.

You recently wrote a very good essay on his work, but something you perhaps don't give obeisance to is Heaney's attachment to what I think you yourself have elsewhere called the matriotism of Ireland, and also a sense of magic and ritual, which you presumably don't share?

As a child I wasn't able to see ghosts, while my brother and my grandmother could. We lived in a very ghostly house, and yet I never saw a ghost. I do disbelieve in the magic in which Yeats dabbled.

But you do credit the notion of a poem being a spell?

Yes, I do. I think, in my own work, 'Nocturne' (in *High Island*) is the least architectural poem, more supplicatory.

Do you especially like working to a commission?

I think it helps to know that there is someone who wants to hear what you have to say. One of the reasons why I've written so little is that I'm very isolated, and when I've gone off to teach in places like Iowa I've not been any less isolated but more so. I *do* have any number of unfinished poems and notes for poems or autobiographical fragments which are still to be worked on. One of the things that held me back is that I have this concept of a poem as a beautiful structure, something you can almost inhabit and that is solid; so that if an utterance or thought I've put down doesn't have that quality I don't see it as a potential poem, it's left in note form. I want to write a prose work, and that's part of my moving to the city, nearer my friends and nearer people who actually read and write poetry.

Is it that the inspiration you've derived from living here has dried up, to put it crudely?

I think my action here has come to an end, building or fishing which involved me with the people of this village. Also, the culture here has changed radically; it's now like an extremely remote suburb of Dublin hooked in to RTE. When I first came here, the tarred road ended at the post office, there were hardly any cars or telephones, and piped water had only just started to come to the houses. The life I wanted then to touch was continuous with the past of a pre-industrial age; it had an oral tradition of poetry kept alive in the conversation of the people. 'Pat Cloherty's Version of *The Maisie*' was the last poem I wrote which came directly out of my life in Cleggan, and it is entirely using the words of the fisherman himself. He died six months after I'd put that poem together, and Pat Concannon is bedridden now. The people I talked to who were brought up in the age of sail are all old or have died. There's a completely new world around us. And I've changed too.

There was a common belief in my family, which many Irish families shared—particularly those with a garrison mentality—that you were likely to waste your life if you stayed in Ireland.

The Sarsfield poem is a celebration of a hero who did nothing but fail at home, all his successes were in foreign countries—he's the hero of emigration. It was generally felt, right up to the 1960s, that there was no future in this country, and I tried to go against this tradition and live at home and not go to seed. Now this country is stronger, richer and more self-assured, with a rising young generation.

How would you characterize your own temperament? Are you withdrawn, meditative and stoical, as you've been described?

I have been in some ways withdrawn, but I'm also very fond of people, and sociable too. I suppose 'stoical' is true; I am austere. I gave up drink a couple of years ago, for instance, and although I'd always enjoyed drinking it wasn't a difficult thing for me to do. I enjoy good health, I go for a run to the beach before breakfast every day, and so I find no pleasure in over-indulging. I'm really an epicurean, I like feeling content.

One thing I don't like is generalizing; I don't like abstract language. Part of my principle in settling in the west is not to generalize or theorize, not to commit myself to any abstract ideals or ideas, because I've seen the horrific consequences of those sorts of commitments. I think the writer is very limited in any political impact he can make upon the world; the strongest impact of all comes from the specific case. In my connection with the tinkers, I've joined no committees and have no general theories about how the problem can be solved. All I know is how a particular family lived and suffered and recovered and was regenerated. A work of art which could show what it was like to be a member of that family would have validity, would be authentic, and I try to apply that test to any poem I write; Tony White was my mentor in that. He was a pupil of Leavis at Cambridge, I had been a pupil of Lewis at Oxford, and I had an awful lot to unlearn and I learned an awful lot from Tony White. I do admire the Cambridge School from the outside.

Do you not feel that in quitting Cleggan you'll discover a tremendous hole in your life?

Well, I've felt for a long time that too strong an attachment to things is bad and that I'd rather be attached to people. I've tended to substitute things for people. My early work is nostalgic for a golden age of the past, and I was looking for that in Connemara. I think it connects with the old Irish myth of Tir na n-Og, the land of everlasting youthfulness. I have at last come awake from that dream. That search for simplicity was a search for childhood; I *did* have a happy childhood. Connemara is certainly the landscape of my imagination, and I'll return to it in my memory, but I don't want to go on living here on my past, and living on my past achievements, such as this granite house. I had built myself into this indestructible situation from which there's no escape except to die. I feel now that my home is in the language.

TOM PAULIN

I want to begin by asking how much you've felt influenced by your background in Belfast, since you've presumably had to work out your own psychological and imaginative freedom?

It may be something to do with the experience of being a kind of immigrant or émigré—if you move out of your own culture and go to a different country you start to realize that many of your actions and the ways you think have been determined for you. I got a similar sense reading Atlas's biography of Delmore Schwartz—Schwartz had a really powerful sense of necessity, mad relatives and so on. In my own case, I've found that a lot of my attitudes were distinctly Protestant, and actually Presbyterian, although I was hardly ever in a Presbyterian Church. I think we're in many ways conditioned by our backgrounds, and you see that very markedly if you have the experience of moving between different cultures and classes. I live as part of an extended Indian family and so I can see some of the ways in which Indian values affect the people born into that culture. I've lived in the north of England, I went to Oxford after Hull, and I've lived in Belfast, and I have the strange experience again and again of hearing people say things that seem to spring right out of their cultural backgrounds. I don't *want* to believe that all our actions and thoughts are determined, and I don't think they are, but I like to think in terms of freedom—inner freedom, the Jamesian idea of freedom—the kind of freedom Nadezhda Mandelstam speaks of in her memoir of Mandelstam.

You do seem to have a deep awareness of the deterministic forces of culture and family. In one of your reviews you draw keen attention to Louis

Simpson's autobiography, Air With Armed Men, *from that angle.*

What interested me about Simpson's autobiography is that as an autobiographer he isn't what I'd call a 'free willer'. He doesn't say 'I made this decision, this choice, and acted on it', but instead he gives the impression that he never made a choice in his life—everything just happened to him. Yet he has the idea of freedom being found in poetry and the voice, a freedom which has been won in the teeth of all the conditioning factors of a peculiar family background—peculiar as all family backgrounds are.

Did you in fact go through a process of dissociation from your family and early religion?

I'd a letter recently from a friend, the historian Roy Foster, and he mentioned 'Atlantic Changelings' and said it struck him reading it that I was a repudiator as only someone who's been through the mill of the Socialist Labour League can be. When I was at school, doing O levels, I belonged to this Trotskyite organization: I felt disaffected from my background, the whole Unionist culture—not that my parents voted Unionist—and I read Orwell in the absorbed way one does at that age. There's a sense, particularly in Irish culture, of deliberate—in fact doctrinaire—disloyalty. I grew up in a culture that was officially Loyalist, but I came to see it was a rotten society: I left it not for political reasons but simply because I wanted to get away from the claustrophobia of that society.

My father's a headmaster and he's a great liberal, I think. He's also in various fascinating ways a utilitarian, which I think an awful but deeply interesting philosophy. So I feel influenced by him—though we've had our differences . . . lots of them. My mother's an Ulster Scot and her family were very strenuous and Victorian—the work ethic, civic responsibility, masses of puritan guilt and all very talkative. Beyond that—my grandfather died when my mother was a girl—there's a whole tradition of Calvinist authoritarianism which fascinates me.

Would you say, in general, that you've had to fight for exemption from a number of cultural forces, then, as much as come to terms with them?

Well, I love Belfast—it's the place I identify with and frequently feel nostaligic for; especially on a rainy day. But what I find at the moment is a real sense of how fundamentally ridiculous and contradictory it is to be an Ulster Protestant. It's a culture which could have dignity, and it had it once—I mean that strain of radical Presbyterianism, free-thinking Presbyterianism, which more or less went underground after 1798. I pretty well despise official Protestant culture, and can't now understand how people can simultaneously wave the Union Jack and yet hate the English, as many Protestants do. I think there really *has* to be a united Ireland, and I don't mean in any way that I'm committed to bloodshed—but it is a fundamentally absurd political state, and it's got to go.

You've written of both Hull and Nottingham as being 'crumbling societies' ... did you perceive a distinct correspondence between your living in those cities and your sense of society in Belfast?

I suppose I've got this daft idea from having read various Russian novels when I was at school, and from reading quite a lot about Russia ... of being fascinated by a sort of twilight *mitteleuropa*—semi-derelict societies, sub-worlds—and that also goes back to having read Orwell's political writings. I've never really thought of those places as having been like the North of Ireland, but there must be something in it.

*'Without Mercy' (*The Strange Museum*) is a poem in which, taking its cue from the underworld journey in* The Aeneid, *what I take to be a suspect hero-figure returns to realize how human values are lost in a polity of rigid conformity—to what extent does that realization represent in some way your own point of view?*

The way that poem came about is that I know a man of some power—a legalistic Scotsman—who reminds me in all sorts of ways of certain Ulster figures; headmasters, politicians. And I'm fascinated by the Calvinist mentality that's represented at its most extreme by someone like Lord Reith. It's a poem that tries to investigate the cultural psychology of that kind of figure. I took the word 'stretch' in the last line—'They are stretched even as the men they stretch'—from a phrase of Reith's, who said he'd felt insufficiently stretched at one point in his life. That seems to me to be a distinctively Calvinistic and individualistic view of experience—and I also associate the word with hanging. I think capital punishment is obscene and revolting—in fact I've a particular childhood memory of a judge who lived opposite my grandmother and how she and I were once at a bus stop on the Malone Road and this judge stopped to offer us a lift. He was an oldish man and I screamed when I saw him—I wouldn't get into the car because I thought this was a man who had hanged people. Anyone who's worked in an institution knows that there are people who have a deep relish of power, and others who don't want it.

Why did you have the protagonist in the poem return through the 'horny gates'—the gates of true dreams—rather than through Aeneas' ivory gates, the gates of false dreams?

The character wakes with an erection, and I'd associate that now with hanging—I don't think I was conscious of it then. I'm really trying to imagine what it's like to be someone in late middle-age, someone who's wielded power, who's Presbyterian—I associate that with justice, not with mercy.

You have a strong sense of the social function of poetry, in the sense that it must be concerned with human values. Yet don't you feel that the poet is in a strange, anomalous position, since he is an individual attending to society while tuning his sensibility in an essentially solitary way?

It's a difficult question. Auden argued that the Romantic poet was essentially an enemy of society. I tend to think that poems of personal emotion have to be struggled for, and when I started writing seriously I didn't think that anyone would be interested in what my feelings were, so I deliberately didn't try and write about them. Perhaps looking at most of my work you wouldn't think I'd any feelings other than bitterness and hatred. You see there's a tradition in English poetry of writing poems of fine and winsome emotions—they're usually set on bridle-paths—and I don't see any point in that. As a subject, personal emotion is somehow subsidized—it's possible at a certain level of prosperity. It wouldn't be a subject you could afford in a country like Poland—it'd seem ridiculous there—and I tend to think of societies like Eastern Europe and Russia where politics are extreme. I can't locate a personal emotion in Ireland which doesn't then become political or social—I'm talking purely about writing here, not about anything else.

In your study of Hardy, Thomas Hardy: The Poetry of Perception, *you seemed to be very exact and engaged in treating the limitations of the positivism or empiricism that he shared with Hume and Comte—limitations in the sense that passive sense-impressions can be sterile. I want to ask, though, don't you feel that a poet owes a distinct duty to the truth of his observations, or do you align yourself with Coleridge in rejecting empirical epistemology for the sake of imaginative freedom?*

I'm very divided about this—obviously it's very puritan to be saying that the senses are misleading and the spirit is free, but on the other hand if one could align the idea of the senses in a more baroque and catholic way, then I'm very attracted to that as a view of life. In the poems at the end of *The Strange Museum* I was in fact trying to work towards that much more integrated, catholic view of experience, and away from the plainness and austerity of setting the spirit above the flesh—if you make this Manichean division, you're bound to think in those terms.

Do you consider yourself very much more an intuitive writer than as any sort of rationalist?

I've met one or two rationalists, and I'm amazed by their view of life, which seems to me to be absolutely bonkers. I do tend to think of writing as being a rare and difficult experience, something that happens to you—you're visited by a cadence and start writing.

I'm thinking of a poem like 'Line on the Grass', which conveys a tactfully understated perception of the North-South border, with careful intimations of its meaning.

Meaning? . . . yes, I was probably much too conscious of trying to state something when I wrote it. The poem's set between Strabane and Lifford where there's a border-crossing. You can't see the border, or touch or taste it, but you know it's there, like a great breach in nature. Beyond that, I'm fascinated by splits between ways of thinking and believing, and I've this collusive wish to try and bridge them, which must link in with a sort of disloyalty.

I try not to write the kind of empirical poem which presents an image of experience and then reflects on that experience. What's so wonderful about parts of *The Prelude* is the way Wordsworth will bind image and reflection together to give you a vision—a vision which takes you beyond what Hume would call sensation-impression-reflection.

Which poem in A State of Justice, *your first book, do you think is the best achieved?*

The one poem I stand by in that book is 'Firelight'. It plays with what's a standard subject—the photograph poem, which is dead and done with now—and so I've tried to leave out mentioning photographs in it. A lot of nineteenth-century writing is taken up with the idea of actually, physically experiencing the supernatural, and therefore with seeing ghosts . . . ghosts if they're visualized become enormously banal. What I tried to catch in 'Firelight' is the idea of a series of afterlives existing as voices, as cadences, which are apprehended at twilight. So it's not a photograph of experience and reflection—it's meant to be a more integral form of being.

As you yourself have written, Hardy, Comte and Leslie Stephen, being agnostic positivists, rule out the possibility of religious faith: do you do so also?

I have absolutely no dogmatic views on the question. I tend to disagree with devoutly religious people—some I respect very much, though—and then I also tend to react against humanists. Since I do believe in the existence of good and evil, I must have some kind of buried religious faith—I don't see how it's possible to believe in the existence of evil without having religious faith. I never go to church, except for weddings and funerals, but I do find that humanism is a very inadequate explanation of experience. To give one example, I saw a girl in India a few years ago who was supposed to have had a curse put on her, to have been taken over by an evil spirit. She's married to my brother-in-law and we were staying in their house. I saw her writhing and cursing under the spell and I naturally sought for all the usual psychosomatic and psychological explanations for what was happening to her, but none of them worked. I find that secular humanism is essentially unimaginative, and I think that mystery and superstition govern our lives in all kinds of ways. I'm fascinated by religious poetry, but that's partly because it's an unfashionable idea of experience.

What you very much applaud in Hardy are the visionary moments of some of his poems: is that something you try to achieve in your own work?

I have tried, but I don't know whether I've ever succeeded. I'm taken by the kind of poetry that does suddenly offer you a vision, and I tried to manage that effect in the last two lines of 'Inishkeel Parish Church':

> There was an enormous sight of the sea,
> A silent water beyond society.

(Though they're destroyed by the fact that they're an inadvertent couplet, and the word 'enormous' sounds too much like Auden and Larkin.)

It's hard to describe—the way you suddenly glimpse into someone else's life ... You know that Clare poem 'To the Snipe'? What I argued for in Hardy was only the very obvious idea that the human personality is unique and the mystery lies in the uniqueness. The trouble with humanism is that it's essentially a very soft philosophy. At work I see people who use the idea of humanity and being human to excuse them from making difficult decisions. There are issues and values and principles beyond humanism, yet where do they lead us? Nadezhda Mandelstam says that if you banish the sacred and say that all values are human values you end up with an immensely cruel political system. On the other hand, if you say that there are values beyond humanism, you're moving in that direction anyway. Maybe sacredness shouldn't be made into an idea, a theoretic value.

Am I right to infer from your own writings that you personally are anti-Romantic, and reluctantly Hobbesian, and that while you affirm a sense of civilitas, *you also allow for the possibility of dissenting voices?*

I think Hobbes's view of life is tremendously dispiriting and I don't *want* to believe in it. My own attitude towards politics and society is, I suppose, a having-it-both-ways view. I've certain ideals about the kind of society I want to live in, which would be a united Ireland with a strong Social Democratic party (I mean the European tradition of social democracy)—but I don't suppose I'll ever live in such a society. That being the case, you have to adjust to the idea of *civilitas*, and also to recognize certain values which exist in English society, like civility and decency, which you don't get anything like as strongly in Ireland. A 'decent' person in Ireland is someone who is kind and sympathetic, perhaps unexpectedly so: this isn't how the word's used in England. What I mean is that there's a very deep Irish desire to push beyond the barriers of the decent and the civil—after all, it was the English who imposed the Pale. In English culture there's an almost mystical idea of not going too far; in more extreme cultures—like Ireland, like Russia—you do go too far, you express 'authentic' emotion. I think many people who admire Lawrence's work aren't really aware that he's outraging various ideals of propriety, tact, civility.

I tend to think that writing comes out of something very messy, the blind man's ditch, or should do.

Do you ever feel that there's a danger that certain poems might become too deliberative; expositions of a pre-formulated view of life? I mean that a poem like 'Purity' can be seen on one level as almost theorematic, since you censure pastoral as a genre for our age?

Actually that poem comes out of an ambivalent feeling I have about Bergman's films, which have the notion of what I've called in the poem 'maritime pastoral'—in other words, they're films with a very puritan idea of experience and of the private life—which I see as being subsidized by the city. This pastoral isn't the English idyll of weekend cottages and glebe lands, but what you have in David Harsent's poetry—stone cottages by fjords or on Baltic islands. What I'm thinking about in the poem is Belfast and also Donegal, where I've spent a lot of time, and then one bright summer morning coming down Belfast Lough on the ferry and seeing a troop-ship going in the opposite direction; and what I'm agonizing about is how the public life—which is cruel and involves seeing people as statistics or mass aggregates—subsidizes certain people who are able to escape it, to get beneath their duvets and supposedly relate to each other. I find a lot of Bergman just stinkingly narcissistic.

Richard Sennett's great book, *The Fall of Public Man*, talks about this huge split between the public and the private life, and how distorting the whole cult of intimate, authentic feeling is, how the privatization of life involves a retreat from any commitment to the public world. In urban planning there's a retreat from inner cities into cosy *gemeinschaft* villages, and you can see this myth presented in a series like *Kojak*. I mean, I like watching it very much, but I'm often struck by the way in which Kojak, who's the representative of *gesellschaft*, the public world, often ends by attending an Italian or Greek wedding—so he's shown in the private world of a minority ethnic community. The connection that's made is a false one, a sentimental one. Another connection is to say that if you stand in front of a beech tree and admire it, what you're really admiring is a vanished form of English society, in that a beech tree presupposes a country house and a very hierarchical society.

Obviously it's awful to bring politics into everything, though you can't help doing so if you live in a totalitarian society, and anyway you can't simply abolish them. I mean, I admire aesthetes and find them very stimulating, but I always have the nagging feeling that they really ought to be thinking about commitment, the public world and politics. Then when I come across what I think are essentially philistine committed writers and critics, I move in the other direction and think of the pure delight of art.

I want to quote the last four stanzas of your fine poem 'The Idea in History', and you might perhaps comment on them:

Out of a soft starfish
The first eye opened
To a pure shrill light.

When the mind grew formal,
Caught in the nets of class,
History became carpets, chairs.

Surfacing like a white fish,
A consciousness is forming.
It travels from bland minsters

To snowcem estates, ideal
Under mountains that were wet,
Bare, until the builders came.

The passage strikes me as a marvellously ambiguous expression of what you actually see as the fitness of human progress and values, while it could also imply a lament for natural landscapes.

It's a terrifying notion that history is a process which is working to articulate an idea, to express that idea in an institution. In the west of Ireland you occasionally come across a co-operative factory or a small housing estate . . . some people, tourists or visitors, would rather just have the wild landscape. But the factory means that the people who live there are going to be more prosperous.

So there's no distinct irony in the poem: snowcem estates are not a regrettable manifestation in your view?

No, not at all.

Though most people might sentimentally opt for the pristine landscape.

Yes, but after that comes the descent into history.

Would it be true to your experience to say that a poem mediates between actual emotional experience and certain determined values: that is, between gut reactions and a decided view of life?

I find that my thinking is fluid, and I'm often out of phase with it. I'll start to write something and then discover what I'd been thinking about. I don't come to a conclusion and then write out of that.

Do you think there's a place for opinions in poetry?

As Yeats said, opinions are a curse—and that's both an aesthetic view and a view of life itself. I really don't know what my opinions are. I tend to have hobby-horses which gallop over me for a while, and then they're replaced by fresh squadrons. An opinion is a dead idea, but then a principle, an ideal, has to have a certain fixity.

A poem such as 'A Partial State' does enunciate a vehement view.

Yes, it does express an opinion about the Unionist state in the North of Ireland. And that is a definite view, though I hope it was discovered in the act of writing. I was partly playing with a phrase of Conor Cruise O'Brien's about irony being 'the weapon of the disarmed'. I think irony at its most extreme is absolutely terrifying. Joyce's irony in *Ulysses* finally abolishes both fact and fiction—it's simultaneously absolutely creative and absolutely destructive. It's curious to find that irony, which is one of the fine and graceful principles of high civilization, can actually be immensely destructive—as it is in Swift. In Poland—which is the country I'm thinking of in 'Where Art is a Midwife'—you have writers and journalists who use irony to communicate essentially libertarian political ideas, ideas they can't spell out directly because of the censors, and so irony is at the service of freedom.

Do you feel there may be a danger that in speaking so forcefully—as you have done in your essays—for an ethic of propriety, tact and civility, you could be misreckoning what you actually know to be a nerveless reality?

I worry about speaking too forcefully, and of course there's a contradiction in speaking brutally in favour of civility. Better that, though, than a dithering limpness. I once reviewed a book which I thought was utterly pornographic and disgusting. The author really hated women, and I pointed this out very harshly. He wrote and complained that I hadn't given him the 'decency' of a review—here was someone with fundamentally indecent views who yet demanded he should be treated decently.

How do you as a poet manage to reconcile and accommodate both imaginative embodiment and social comment?

One commonly thinks of imagination and society as being at opposite poles, but if you read early Auden you have the sense of the actual world being haunted by political and ideological ghosts. At times—especially in *The Age of Anxiety*—Auden will look at reality like a sociologist. How do you heal the breach between an imagination of the world and the world of social facts? I think it happens in certain historical situations—when things are moving very quickly and you're perceiving things in a way that makes them become luminous, mysterious, strange. I get this sense near the border—not the intensity of the historical process, though, just stasis, stasis. It always feels like mid-afternoon at the border—very stale and drab.

Do you want to make your readers reflect as much as to feel?

There's this phrase that Wordsworth and Coleridge use, the 'despotism of the eye', and it's even more despotic nowadays. We overvalue the visual, we demand that poetry must have visual images. I'm very suspicious of this and of the way many critics value poems not for their cadences, how they sound, but for their visual images.

If I pose the notions of contemplation and vision on the one hand, and definition, analysis and diagnosis on the other, would you be content to acknowledge that your poetry largely falls into the latter group?

I would love to think that an analysis of whatever the subject is would lead to contemplation; but of course the idea of contemplation is, I suppose, essentially quietistic. Although my ambition is to be responsible in a way, to give a sense of history and of society, what I really want to do is to punch holes in history—tunnel through it—in order to get out into a kind of freedom which is contemplation and vision. To give an example, the poem I've written or pinched called 'Trotsky in Finland' comes out of a chapter in Trotsky's autobiography, and it struck me that the quality of his writing had certain literary associations. The description of the landscape—a winter's afternoon just before he went to help lead the 1905 revolution—is like one of those moments in Tolstoy which come across with an intense freshness. We know that Tolstoy read Schopenhauer, and these visionary descriptions of landscape are moments which Schopenhauer calls *Vorstellung*. Now if you're a Marxist you say that the admiration of landscape is a form of bourgeois consumption, but that's rubbish because the way in which Tolstoy conveys landscape goes beyond that. And so, too, with this moment in Trotsky. His description of the guest-house, the writer and his mistress, evokes a kind of Chekhovian flimsiness. Again, the moment when he hears the news of the strikes spreading and calls for horses is a Byronic moment—does that mean that

Trotsky conceived of himself as someone who made a conscious decision, since we think of Byron as a Napoleonic figure, the incarnation of Will, dominating history?

The point about literary parallels is the same as, say, drawing a parallel between a conversation you happen to overhear and a play by Pinter—the reason you make the comparison is because art is freedom. By taking a historical event and translating it into imaginative terms or drawing imaginative parallels with it, you're suddenly transforming it perhaps into the world of myth—certainly into the realm of what is fictive. And by doing that you are actually punching a hole in the historical process and opening up an imaginative view of it. On the other hand, when you start mythologizing political events something very dangerous happens—you forget about the human suffering involved and see the events simply in terms of what's glorious and heroic and mythic. It's what Yeats means when he talks about too many sacrifices making a stone of the heart. And just as the Flaubertian sacrifice of life for art's sake makes a stone of the heart, so the intransigent nationalist sacrifice of the individual life or happiness for the sake of the national ideal hardens the heart.

And yet is one sure that Trotsky treats that incident in his memoirs with the amount of irony and reflection that you bring to bear?

I'm convinced he did—he was a man of the most extraordinary literary sensibility. It's a fascinating passage: I think it's very self-conscious and ironic. He's describing a moment of pure being, a private moment outside the process of history. Trotsky also mentions someone he knew who was obsessed with puns, and I associate that naturally with Joyce. They're rather similar figures, Trotsky and Joyce—I mean they both went into exile in order to destroy and recreate their societies. *Ulysses* is a kind of bomb—the last great novel in English, the novel that reduced the English novel after it to a minor form. It's very creative and very destructive.

I gather that you feel critical of solipsistic or self-referring behaviour: is that to say that you think of poems as possessing an impersonal power?

Perhaps it's all to do with treatment. I put that poem, 'Man

With Hookah', towards the end of *The Strange Museum* because I was trying to move towards a view of art as self-delighting. It's certainly a characteristic of Indian culture that people don't think of ends and means, and they don't feel guilt.

The posture I discern in the poem is that you feel rather beguiled by this pacific life, indulgent to its ease and mystery, as you suggest.

A general characteristic of Indian life is to hang about and enjoy yourself. Everything is spirit—movement and stillness come together. When Indian women are cooking and they lift a pot or something they give the impression of lifting the object for the act itself, to savour the object or the act for itself. It's a very laid-back feeling . . . extremely graceful and non-utilitarian.

To what extent to do think 'Man With Hookah' might mark a new departure in your work?

Well, I thought I'd more or less disappeared into this aestheticism, but then the last poem I wrote—a sequence called 'The Book of Juniper' [*TLS* 8 February 1980]—is eventually political.

'The Garden of Self-Delight', on the other hand, does strike me as being censorious towards an aestheticism which I suppose took that almost mystical cast in 'Man with Hookah' . . . ironically, perhaps.

I do link mysticism and aestheticism, and I thought 'The Garden of Self-Delight' wasn't censorious at all. I remember years ago this very hot day and wandering through a Roman garden on the Adriatic coast of Yugoslavia, the smells of bay leaves and pungent herbs. Of course, I think there *is* finally a law which cuts across our Bacchic pleasures, but if only there wasn't . . . And I think the poem's saying how wonderful it would be to belong to a place of southern pleasures.

So the poem is finally a circumspect assent to the possibility of writing an apolitical poem, undaunted by anything like 'relevance'?

Relevance is a gruelling and philistine ethic—those people who *insist* that art must be relevant actually hate art—and yet in certain societies it would be very difficult to indulge in the notion of art for art's sake with any kind of cogency.

While there may be no particular virtue in using obliqueness or evasiveness for its own sake in poetry, would it disturb you to be tagged with certain con-

cerns and attitudes—I mean, the sort of labelling critics like to go in for?

If I were to be identified with a particular political attitude or philosophy, I'd be upset. I'm not a Marxist, for example, and I don't have any ideological axe to grind.

Would you like the critical reception of your work to set as much store by your techniques as by the ideas you express in poetry?

I hope the two can't be separated, but maybe they can. I see ideas as spirit developing and expressing itself in form. Long after writing it, I thought in the last poem of *The Strange Museum*, 'A Lyric Afterwards', I'd managed to combine stress metre and quantitative metre—at least I hope that's true.

Can you say what the notion of a poetic voice means to you?

Most of the reviews of my first book quite properly pointed out that there were a series of received voices in it, and I have to squirm when I think how that parodic element enters into a number of those poems. I've a poor memory for faces, but I have an obsession with voices. I think that comes partly from having read Robert Frost's few pages on 'sentence sounds' years and years ago, and that Edward Thomas poem, 'The Owl', then. I think there are roughly two traditions in English poetry: one is Parnassian, or at least melodious, and the other's Gothic. The Gothic really begins with Wyatt and has a kind of thorny texture. The main inspiration of Gothic is the quirky individuality of the voice, and that's what fascinates me. Mandelstam, whom I revere, composed by lying on a sofa and voicing the words as they came to him—his lips had to move, and he composed above all for sound. Surely the imagination is a voice that visits you and tells you, very gently, what to write? It may be an act of faith (I can only read Mandelstam in translation), but always I seem to hear this fragrant, mysterious voice.

Would you agree that there seems to be almost a deliberative balance of themes in your first book, A State of Justice*—one of them being the recognition of the blind, authoritarian tyranny of certain social and political forces? Is it fair, do you think, for me to see the book almost equally divided between negative or critical responses—in poems like 'Under the Eyes', 'Cadaver Politic', 'The Hyperboreans' and 'Provincial Narratives'—and* *poems which are much more positive or affirmative, such as 'A New Society'? . . . That may be a reductive summary.*

It's rough and raw, that volume. Certainly I sometimes try to imagine better societies—there's a dream, in 'The Hyperboreans', of Ireland as a kind of Yugoslavia.

The poem called 'Under the Roof' presumably derives directly from your experience of living in Nottingham?

It's a monologue; the voice in the poem isn't actually mine but an attempt to communicate a particular type of personality, a type of masculine mind, and also a mind that's trapped in the notion that sense-experience is all there is. The attitude is supposed to be bitter, though the social detail must be familiar to anyone who's lived in a bedsit.

Is the last poem in A State of Justice, *'Also an Evasion', meant to hark back to earlier poems in the book, and perhaps to characterize the whole volume?*

Yes, its sterility is meant to tie in.

Can you describe how you feel you've developed in your second volume, The Strange Museum*?*

I spent a long, agonizing time revising and shaping the volume, trying to make it cohere. The spirit hungers for form and yet so often that form goes dead. From the first poem to the last there's meant to be a kind of parabola—where do you find the living form that expresses the spirit?

In 'A Lyric Afterwards', do you mean to endorse an exclusive commitment to personal relationships?

No, I can't make the separation of personal relationships from everything else.

Can you explain your sense of the title-poem, 'The Strange Museum', perhaps with particular reference to the last stanza—which I take to be an unironic assent to the society you now live in?

> *. . . I woke in a tennis suburb.*
> *History could happen elsewhere, I was free now*
> *in a neat tame place whose gods were milder.*
> *A cold dawn, but a different season.*
> *There was the rickety fizz of starlings*

trying to sing, and a grey tenderness.
I was happy then, knowing the days had changed
and that you would come back here, to this room.
You were the season, beyond winter, the first freshness.

It's a personal poem, but set in a particular society—Belfast. The experience behind it is a road accident in which my wife was badly injured. In the lines you quote I'm talking about England—the accident happened in Ireland—and saying it's much milder as a culture. Earlier in the poem I'm trying to imagine the past as a fixed museum and so I'm trying to get out of history—into the banal pleasantries of suburbia which it's a mistake to undervalue.

A last question: do you feel a sense of community with certain other writers?

Obviously with Douglas Dunn, my first literary friend and a great inspirer. And with the community represented by Frank Ormsby's anthology, *Poets from the North of Ireland*. That community has to be an *imaginative* one because otherwise a curious thing happens—art gets used to bolster the state. I saw this happen at a conference not long ago where certain writers from the North were held up by the chairman of the Northern Ireland Arts Council as examples of the essential health of the state. He would have been better employed offering us as symptoms of disease in the body politic. I go down to London now and then and that's fun—seeing Craig Raine always cheers me up. I feel part of a community in Nottingham now, and that's nice. It reminds me of Belfast.

CRAIG RAINE

If we can start by talking a little about your background and early life . . . were you in fact a middle-class child?

No, working-class. I was born in 1944 in Shildon in County Durham—it used to be a thriving mining and railway town, but now it exists (more or less) around a smallish industrial estate. My father's mother was a variety artiste, a singer and dancer: her stage name was Queenie Ray, and she once did a Command Performance for Edward VII. Her husband, my grandfather, came from a good family (bishops, barristers and mayors) but he was the black sheep, a stage-door Johnnie. He ended up on the boards himself for a time, married my grandmother, then worked on the railways. My father worked on the railways, too, and mastered a variety of trades—painter, decorator, plumber, electrician and glazier. But he was really a boxer. He started fighting exhibition bouts when he was seven, with his brother, and turned professional when he was sixteen. In those days, of course, the purses were so small he needed another job.

He was quite a successful boxer: he fought for the featherweight title of Great Britain and claims to be the only man who ever put the holder, Mickey Maguire, down on the canvas. All the same, he lost the fight. His father, who was in his corner, threw in the towel. After that he was reinstated amateur. My parents furnished their house with boxing prizes—canteens of cutlery, clocks, and so on. As an amateur, he fought twice for England. In 1937 he fought against Germany and beat the Olympic Games winner, Otto Kästner. Ribbentrop presented the cup. The fight was apparently a tremendous blood-bath. My father was split across both eyes from two butts: he says that when you're cut like that your eyelids drop down on to your cheek, so you look through the gap. My father is a great raconteur and I've heard this story so many times I know it by heart. The referee wanted to stop the fight in the German's favour after the first round, but my father's response was to say, 'I'll beat this bugger with two broken legs!' Since my father had been a pro and knew all the dirty tricks, he simply gave his opponent the heel of the glove (you use the laces like a cheese-grater). Kästner's cheek was slashed so that you could see his teeth through the hole. Amazingly, the fight went the distance—they weren't readily stopped in those days. It was impossible afterwards to distinguish the Red Rose of England on his white vest, so much blood had bounced from one man to the other. That's part of my father.

In 1940, shortly after he'd joined the RAF, he was blown up (in a Glasgow munitions factory, we think) and disabled—he suffers from epilepsy caused by a chunk of shrapnel. He's lived on a war disability pension ever since.

The other interesting thing about him is that he's a practising spiritualist and a faith-healer. Basically, he's a self-taught physiotherapist. If someone comes with cancer or a broken arm, my father sends them to hospital, but he's terribly good at fixing slipped discs or cartilages. He cured my brother of polio: that's how he discovered that he could do it. My brother had been discharged from hospital paralysed down the right side in about 1946, and my father fed and re-educated the wasted muscles. He did the same for another boy, too. He's a colourful character: although his boxing stories are all incredibly violent he's, paradoxically, an extremely gentle man.

My mother, who is about seven years younger than he, is a quiet woman who married this local hero. She's a classic Lawrentian mother who wanted her children to do well, and so my brother and I didn't go to the local grammar school but got scholarships to Barnard Castle School, where we boarded. She took in sewing so that we could have pocket-money and clothes. She's a remarkable, intelligent, interesting woman. My father's past is now arranged into anecdotes—which is an art of sorts—not raw material at all. My mother has never crystallized her memories, so that, as a writer, I'm much more able to use what I learn from her. Her memories are purer, unfinished, evocative and untouched by narrative.

Do you feel you were influenced by them both equally?

Equally, probably, but it's hard to say precisely. I'm not very sure what I'm like. I recognize shared qualities, not all of them good.

Were you brought up to practise a religion?

My mother was a Catholic, and children of a mixed marriage had to be brought up in the Catholic faith. I wasn't a religious boy, though for a year in about 1953 I was an altar-boy and went to Mass every day. I was tremendously keen on the rig—the surplice and cassock, the whole ceremonial—and I adored being praised. I remember going to Buckingham Palace with my mother; I made her wait six hours to see the Queen. While we waited, I told my rosary with totally bogus piety.

It was vanity and narcissism?

Yes, absolutely. My public school was Anglican, so the Catholics and Jews didn't go to chapel: I learned about skiffle when others were learning about God, and we smoked a lot. On Sundays we were allowed to go to the local Catholic church. In fact, we used to stand outside smoking and then slip into the back of the church near the end of Mass, usually in time to avoid putting anything in the second collection. The priest, Father Ploughman, was always delighted to see us and would give us half-a-crown each: it's a shaming, amusing memory.

Did you have a smooth academic run and go straight to Oxford?

In my year two people went to Cambridge, and I went to Oxford, and that was reckoned to be pretty good for the school. It wasn't academically distinguished, though I was well taught: my English master, a man named Arnold Snodgrass, had taught with Auden—at the same prep school, I think—and was himself a formidable man. We mostly ignored the syllabus and studied his own enthusiasms: a lot of modern drama, Beckett, Osborne, Pinter, Wesker. I remember we prepared Milton for 'A' level in one double period. I started writing poetry for the same reason that I liked being an altar boy, it appealed to my vanity; I was doing something that nobody else was doing in the sixth form. I read the *Four Quartets* when I was sixteen, and impressed myself no end. Not that I understood them, but I thought, 'This is poetry, something no one can understand,' so I wrote reams of nonsense. I sent two poems to Philip Toynbee at the *Observer*—because he was the only person I'd ever heard of—and he replied, saying that they weren't much good and that I ought to use rhyme and learn the craft. It was an extremely kind letter; they really were dreadful poems. I showed some of my poetry to my English master, who pronounced it 'pimply Dylan Thomas'. He also said I should learn to rhyme and that I should stop using 'I' in my poems; and I still find it awkward to do that. It's an odd thing, in my first book I don't feature as a character in my poems the way other poets do in theirs.

And you attribute that to being told not to use 'I' in your first efforts at verse?

Yes, partly. It was an accident, but quite a good one: it makes one different from other people. My English master was a tough, very critical man. He enjoyed intellectual iconoclasm and was, I remember, quite pleased once when I expressed myself rather coolly about Molière to my headmaster. I went on to Exeter College, and spent most of my three years trying to get my schoolboy poems printed. I wrote hardly any poems as an undergraduate; I wrote very bad short stories instead, all derived from Hemingway—every third word was 'and' . . .

Did any particular tutor influence you?

I was taught by Jonathan Wordsworth, who had a strong, charismatic personality, and as a result I wanted to be a don. I took a B. Phil. in Nineteenth-Century and Twentieth-Century Studies, which I enjoyed. At the same time, I always thought of myself as being a poet—in a separate part of my head . . . Even though I'd written so little and none of it any good. I started to write again to justify this idea of myself to a girl I was keen on. Meanwhile, my donnish bit started a doctorate on Coleridge's philosophy and I was doing some teaching. I taught Martin Amis, who went on to the *TLS* and asked me to do some reviewing.

What with that and writing poetry my doctorate rather went by the board. There's a hole in my *curriculum vitae*. I've had a series of lectureships—at Lincoln College, Exeter College twice, and then at Christ Church, for three years. But they were all temporary, and now I'm editing *Quarto*. I enjoyed teaching very much, but I'm easily bored by the idea of research into minor literature.

Are you interested in making a book of your essays and reviews?

Well, I've written some long essays on Stevens, on Joyce, on Eliot, on Auden, on Kipling, on Donne, which are probably book-length *in toto*. But I'd like to rewrite and rethink and add to them—otherwise it's a chancy enterprise. Seamus Heaney is publishing a collection of his essays, and he was joking about titles. I suggested 'Siftings', and Heaney replied, 'Ah, yes, Hopkins's "soft sift in an hour-glass",' but I said, 'No, actually I was thinking of Eliot, "and let their liquid siftings fall"!' So even a title is dangerous.

Do you think you have a philosophy of life in general, or are your ideas more experiential than categorical?

No, I don't have a philosophy of life. I think Oxford taught me not exactly scepticism but an argumentative open-ness. I really have a free-floating acceptance of possibilities; I don't think anything is unthinkable; I admire Arnold's polemics for impartiality.

Taking up your cue from Arnold and thinking about touchstones, do you feel you owe any debts to specific works of art or philosophy, poems or poets?

I'm fond of painting, and Picasso is an influential figure. I was struck by his free versions of great paintings from the past: Velasquez; his two versions of *Le Déjeuner sur l'herbe*; a Delacroix. That's what I was doing in 'Kublaikansky'; setting it in Russia to allow myself a certain amount of freedom. Picasso's cubism partly stands behind the 'Yellow Pages' poems in *The Onion, Memory*. I wondered what the poetic equivalent would be. By using fractured images he'd broken the rule of the fixed viewpoint: the equivalent in poetry might be to mix your metaphors. At the same time, the most successful of his cubist pictures were those that depicted something so familiar (like the human face) that one could distort a great deal without losing the fundamental sense of it. By analogy, I thought subjects like a butcher or a barber could be bombarded with images from a thousand different directions without destroying the unity of the impression. In any case, as I wrote them, they turned out to have their own unities and narratives anyway. All writing is producing a royal flush from the confused hand of jacks, clubs, diamonds and hearts that life deals you.

I like the density of Hopkins. My earliest influence, strangely enough, was Robert Lowell. I don't think it shows in anything I've published, though 'Gethsemane' owes something to 'Skunk Hour'. The writer I most admire is Joyce: I take *Ulysses* everywhere with me in case I get knocked down by a bus. He's a writer who can make anything interesting. I'm surprised no one's remarked on his influence. The first of the 'Yellow Pages' poems was 'The Grocer', and it began in competition with Joyce's passage about Bloom buying a kidney:

> His hand accepted the moist tender gland and slid it into a sidepocket. Then it fetched up three coins from his trousers' pocket and laid them on the rubber prickles. They lay, were read quickly and quickly slid, disc by disc, into the till.

One of Joyce's pupils in Trieste recalled that Joyce used to make his students go away and describe, say, an oil lamp: the student coined the phrase 'descriptive lust' to evoke Joyce's aim. That's what I'm interested in. All the writers I admire have it. Heaney has a poem of which the first line is '"Description is revelation!"', and I believe that.

But description or impressionism is a fairly modest ambition, isn't it?

Well, that depends on how good you are—but all I'm saying is that it's a starting-point, a *sine qua non*. You hoard images, and wait to see what they suggest and how they work in the poem. My poems aren't written by a magpie collecting fragments; they work as wholes. They relate to present some argument. I don't think I'm a *dull* person, but what interests me in writing are the things the poem itself suggests (under authorial supervision, of course) . . . you may start to write a poem about one thing and then discover that it's about something else. If you're sensible you listen to the poem. I wish critics did, too. Good critics always take a *single* poem (at some stage in their review) and show how it works. Bad ones never do. It's a good rule of thumb.

Would it be true to say, though, that you regard the phenomenal world as a fiction to be sported with, analysed, diagnosed?

I suppose you're referring to my allusion to Berkeley in 'An Enquiry Into Two Inches of Ivory'. I don't believe there's any right way to look at the world—I mistrust prescriptivism. Berkeley happened to suit my purpose in that particular poem . . . But I don't believe the world's a fiction. Sometimes I'm a Johnsonian, kicking stones. It all depends . . . on the poem, I suppose. Either way, I want to place, describe, the world exactly. Images allow you to quote the world; you can quote phenomena through images.

And yet an image can form a barrier between object and apprehension.

So people say . . . these days. I'm content to agree with Eliot on simile and metaphor (in his *Dante* essay): 'The purpose of this type of simile is solely to make us *see more definitely* the scene which Dante has put before us in the preceding lines.' Except that I think simile can be as expansive as metaphor.

Would you affirm Wallace Stevens's suggestion that 'a sense of reality keen enough to be in excess of the normal sense of reality creates a reality of its own'?

Evidently some of my reviewers think I leave the world behind, but that's not my intention. Maybe they have a dull sense of reality. I read the world like a thriller—endlessly exciting, mysterious and natural. I don't see why I should cater for their text-book world with the answers at the back (i.e. the glum moral statement at the end of a poem).

Do you have a sense of your work as having the function of arbitration—judging the world—sometimes censorious, sometimes compassionate?

I think poetry—at least in this country—is often very pious; people don't admit to feeling certain things. Poetry is impoverished when reduced to socially acceptable statements. One of the reasons I admire Berryman, for instance, is that he is quite prepared to own up to all sorts of things. Berryman is a religious poet, who praises God for producing the sun but he *also* knows that God produced the boring old moon. And who else has written about diarrhoea? Second-rate poets limit themselves to the great safe themes . . .

Would you actually acknowledge that your vision of the world is figured on a keen sense of regret, a sense of the defunctive and futile, or a lament for a lost Arcadia?

Nothing as programmatic as that. I'm interested in all those things, but one's subject matter is partly dictated by what the poem is doing, and partly by what happens to you in life. Your poems change because, for example, you've had children—hardly ever because you're reacting to what critics have said, as John Bayley implied in his very kind review in the *TLS*. All the same, I was a bit baffled when reviewers of my first book found it chilly . . . Michael Longley distinguished himself and earned my everlasting gratitude by pointing out how tender it was.

Carrying on from the point that some critics have found your work artificial, would you feel that an art of ingenuity is necessarily, and justly, irresponsible, or would you profess that your work has fidelity to mood, emotion, scene, or style of mind? I mean, your images can seem to be capricious.

I'm fascinated by your use of the word 'irresponsible', which—in this case—usually means irresponsible to received opinion. There's always a strong pressure on the poet to repeat what others have said. On the whole I'm interested in entirely original images. For instance, I like Donne, but I find him uneven. Some of Donne simply plunders a tired old word-hoard where every image is dog-eared. In 'The Butcher' I describe the man very carefully. For me, 'careful' also means full of care: it's a tender, teasing poem—the way you tease someone you like. The poem isn't merely ingenious: it's true—butchers do flirt with their customers. So I am being faithful to what's in front of me. I'm not an introverted person, I hardly ever think about what's going on inside me; I prefer to discover it through looking very hard at something else. I keep my eye on the object; I'm responsible to it; I respond to it.

Is it true to your experience, though, to say that sense-experience is somehow disavowed or discredited in the act of writing?

I'm not self-conscious about art, and I don't have the kind of angst that Geoffrey Hill and Peter Porter suffer, both of whom feel guilty about writing. Writing is a perfectly natural activity: it's publication they're really worried about. Writing is the slavey of sense-experience—unpaid but eager to serve.

Would you accept the critical view that your work is essentially an art of the visual?

I think it's aural too, like the beginning of my poem 'Demolition with Tobacco Speck'—'Hic, haec, hoc—the dead language/of bricks . . .' But, in any case, it's not just a question of taking clever snapshots; it's a question of arranging the snapshots so that they present some implicit argument.

Do you begin each poem with a sure sense of subject and range, or is it supplied in the act of writing?

On the whole, the latter. But sometimes it's a subject.

But you work more from the perceptual than from the imaginative?

If you want an entirely imaginative poet, you'd choose someone like James Fenton, who creates very exciting, extraordinary poems. But I really don't accept or understand the distinction.

Are you scared of virtuosity, and could you perhaps comment on how you see the relationship between wit and seriousness?

If you say imagination, craft and skill, instead of 'virtuosity', the question evaporates. I try to give people as much ambrosia as they can eat. Naïve readers enjoy my work enormously. Donne's *Anniversaries* are full of wit and yet their argument is a *contemptus mundi*. No contradiction. I think my second book is sombre but also witty, and for me there's no conflict.

Do you have a sense of your audience?

I think you create the taste by which you are enjoyed, as Wordsworth said. (It's awful to hark to Wordsworth and Arnold and Eliot all the time, but who else does one hark to?—not J. C. Squire or Walter de la Mare.) All the same, you make allowances for your audience. You learn that poetry is not just a private act but also a public one.

You'd underwrite Stevens's notion that the poet 'fulfils himself as he sees his imagination become the light in the minds of others'?

Yes, I think that happens. I think a lot of young poets have been excited by what I've done.

Don't you feel that a poet is in danger of losing in depth of feeling what he gains in terms of flashing intuitions and shocks of recognition?

Currently we have a very crude view of what constitutes feeling; there's a terrible dead orthodoxy about what poets are allowed to feel. I noticed it particularly in reviews of Christopher Reid's book *Arcadia*: critics say that he's unfeeling. Chris *is* more dandified than I am, but his poems are full of feeling: he's constantly yelping that he loves things.

Well, how do you react to the fact that you've been teamed with Christopher Reid? Do you feel a kinship with his work, or do you feel that your techniques and attitudes are different from his?

Chris is an old pupil of mine, a contemporary of Martin Amis, and my oldest friend. There are similarities and differences between Chris and myself as obvious as the similarities and differences between Donne and Marvell. I think he's a very fine poet indeed. He has an impeccable ear for breaking a line.

Is your own approach to poetry postulated at all on the difference between an Ideal and the everyday world?

I think it is to some extent in my long sequence 'Anno Domini', which takes as its structural basis the life of Christ but is in fact the biography of a faith-healer: sometimes he speaks, and sometimes other people. In one sense the poem is about failure, about a faith-healer who's considerably less famous than Christ was—largely by accident—but it's also about poetry. I've mentioned that my father is a faith-healer, and he does go around—as in the section called 'Sunblest Bread & Two Tail-Ends of Cod'—giving Extra-Strong Mints to kids and saying 'Will you be in my gang?' and 'Do you want a lion-tamer?' So it's about my father, but it's more or less about the imagination: all the miracles in the poem are imaginative miracles. In Section V, for instance, if you see a man with Hutchinson's Career, as I have, in terms of a one-man band, in a sense he's 'cured' by that. Yet the 'cure' illustrates a gap between the ideal and the real world. But the gap doesn't apply everywhere in my poetry.

Can you explain why you chose the unrhymed couplet as your preferred form in A Martian Sends a Postcard Home, *and your general sense of rhythm?*

Technique is something you learn in order to reach a point where you're writing what you want with the minimum of interference. The unrhymed couplet interested me as something in which I could write fluently. Any verse, however, with a fair amount of freedom in it is actually much harder to write than strict verse. Edward Lucie-Smith said that my poems are not rhythmically inert but are all written to the same tune, and I thought it quite a shrewd remark. That's one's style, one's voice: and it's hard to find in different forms. I tried unrhymed quatrains—feeling, groping for each line. Then my wife pointed out that my measure was roughly six syllables per line—once the pattern became mechanical, instead of intuitive, I lost interest. But the unrhymed couplet *had* interested me to the extent that I rewrote some of the poems for my first book, which had originally been in rhymed quatrains or some other form.

Perhaps you could say something about your work in progress, and your ambitions? Has the sense of sombreness and mortality become the main drift of your work?

I'd like to write more, but I don't want to repeat myself.

But the work you've done so far would suggest that you couldn't readily undertake an extended argumentative or reflective poem?

I don't think one can predict. As for extended sequences, I have written one in 'Anno Domini'. Obviously what I like doing is seeing things very clearly and working out their implications in a poem, and that's the way I am. When I went for a walk with my daughter earlier today, for example, I saw two cricket sight-screens as a couple reading newspapers: that's the way it struck me, and I'll never lose that way of seeing things. I wouldn't necessarily go along with Larkin's notion that there's no need to develop; I think you develop anyway, naturally. Larkin's view of death has changed radically, for instance; he's grown older.

In a Poetry Book Society Bulletin you remark that in A Martian Sends a Postcard Home *you've deliberately chosen a neutral, objective tone which should not be mistaken for lack of feeling. Perhaps we could end with a comment on that remark?*

What I mean is that I'm not interested in ingratiating myself with the reader as an entirely sensitive, right-minded, liberal poet who could figure in the *New Statesman* and not shame anybody. I'm not interested in writing poems which end with thumping statements; I'm interested in making objects. I think poems are machines in the sense that Baudelaire called Delacroix's paintings machines; they have to work as artistic objects.

BIBLIOGRAPHY

DOUGLAS DUNN

Terry Street, Faber, London, 1969.
The Happier Life, Faber, London, 1972.
Love or Nothing, Faber, London, 1974.
Barbarians, Faber, London, 1979.

THOM GUNN

Fighting Terms, Faber, London, 1954; 2nd edn, 1962.
The Sense of Movement, Faber, London, 1957.
My Sad Captains, Faber, London, 1961.
Positives, with Ander Gunn, Faber, London, 1966.
Touch, Faber, London, 1967.
Moly, Faber, London, 1971.
Jack Straw's Castle, Faber, London, 1976.
Selected Poems 1950–1975, Faber, London, 1979.

SEAMUS HEANEY

Death of a Naturalist, Faber, London, 1966.
Door into the Dark, Faber, London, 1969.
Wintering Out, Faber, London, 1972.
North, Faber, London, 1975.
Stations, Ulsterman Publications, Belfast, 1975.
Field Work, Faber, London, 1979.

Preoccupations: Selected Prose 1968–1978, Faber, London, 1980.
Selected Poems 1965–1975, Faber, London, 1980.

GEOFFREY HILL

For the Unfallen: Poems 1952–1958, Deutsch, London, 1959.
King Log, Deutsch, London, 1968.
Mercian Hymns, Deutsch, London, 1971.
Tenebrae, Deutsch, London, 1978.
Brand ('A Version for the English Stage'), Heinemann, in association with the National Theatre, London, 1978.

THOMAS KINSELLA

Poems, The Dolmen Press, Dublin, 1956.
Another September, The Dolmen Press, Dublin, 1958.
Downstream, The Dolmen Press, Dublin, 1962.
Wormwood, The Dolmen Press, Dublin, 1966.
Nightwalker and Other Poems, The Dolmen Press, Dublin; OUP, London, 1968.
The Tain (translation), The Dolmen Press, Dublin, 1969; OUP, London, 1970.
Butcher's Dozen: A Lesson for the Octave of Widgery, Peppercanister 1, Dublin, 1972.
A Selected Life, Peppercanister 2, Dublin, 1972.
Notes from the Land of the Dead and Other Poems, Knopf, New York, 1973.
New Poems, The Dolmen Press, Dublin, 1973.
Selected Poems 1956–1968, The Dolmen Press, Dublin, 1973.
Vertical Man: a sequel to A Selected Life, Peppercanister 3, Dublin, 1973.
The Good Fight: a poem for the tenth anniversary of the death of John F. Kennedy, Peppercanister 4, Dublin, 1973.
One, Peppercanister 5, Dublin, 1974.
Fifteen Dead, The Dolmen Press in association with OUP, Dublin, 1979.

One and Other Poems, The Dolmen Press in association with OUP, Dublin, 1979.

PHILIP LARKIN

The North Ship (first published 1945), Faber, London, 1966.
Jill (novel, 1946), Faber, London, 1975.
A Girl in Winter (novel, 1947), Faber, London, 1975.
The Less Deceived, The Marvell Press, Hessle, York, 1955, 1977.
The Whitsun Weddings, Faber, London, 1964.
High Windows, Faber, London, 1974.

PAUL MULDOON

New Weather, Faber, London, 1973.
Mules, Faber, London, 1977.
Why Brownlee Left, Faber, London, 1980.

RICHARD MURPHY

The Last Galway Hooker, The Dolmen Press, Dublin, 1961.
Sailing to an Island, Faber, London, 1963.
The Battle of Aughrim, Faber, London, 1968.
High Island, Faber, London, 1974.
Selected Poems, Faber, London, 1979.

TOM PAULIN

A State of Justice, Faber, London, 1977.
The Strange Museum, Faber, London, 1980.

CRAIG RAINE

The Onion, Memory, OUP, Oxford, 1978.
A Martian Sends a Postcard Home, OUP, Oxford, 1979.